# To Fall in Love, Drink This

*A Wine Writer's Memoir*

## Alice Feiring

Scribner

New York   London   Toronto   Sydney   New Delhi

Scribner
An Imprint of Simon & Schuster, Inc.
1230 Avenue of the Americas
New York, NY 10020

First Scribner trade paperback edition August 2022

For information about special discounts for bulk purchases, please contact Simon & Schuster Special Sales at 1-866-506-1949 or business@simonandschuster.com.

The Simon & Schuster Speakers Bureau can bring authors to your live event. For more information or to book an event, contact the Simon & Schuster Speakers Bureau at 1-866-248-3049 or visit our website at www.simonspeakers.com.

Manufactured in the United States of America

1 3 5 7 9 10 8 6 4 2

Library of Congress Cataloging-in-Publication Data has been applied for.

ISBN 978-1-9821-7676-1
ISBN 978-1-9821-7678-5 (ebook)

Also by Alice Feiring

*The Battle for Wine and Love*
*Naked Wine*
*For the Love of Wine*
*The Dirty Guide to Wine*
*Natural Wine for the People*

For Becky Wasserman-Hone

# Contents

# CONTENTS

# Introduction

My ninety-eight-year-old mother never seems to stop asking me, "This is what you do for a living? Tell people what to drink?"

God knows I've tried to explain to her what kind of work I do. "Ethel," I'll say, "while there's nothing wrong with being a wine critic, that's not my job." And then I'll go on and on about mysticism and metaphor. I think the last time I tried that, she just laughed.

How can I explain to her, a person who understands only sweet, cheap kosher wine, that my trajectory has been not so much to direct wine lovers to life-changing bottles but to expose the industry's abuses and to explore understanding wine's spiritual underpinnings? I mean, what was this fermented grape juice all about? When I think of it, which I often do, I stand head bent in awe. When attacked by the Turks, Georgian soldiers went into battle with a vine clipping near their breast; should they die on the field, a grapevine would take root through their heart. Even if that story was nothing more than local mythology, the love behind the myth begs for attention: Why have cultures lived and died for the right to farm, make, and drink wine? Why does almost every culture have a relationship to wine? Why do people like me continue to ponder it, obsess about it, drink it, write about it? One writes to figure out the truth. Wine is the metaphor that I never cease to find meaning in.

The wine odds were against me. If you ask Ethel (go ahead, look up "Jewish mother" in the dictionary, you'll see her name right there), I was supposed to be a doctor like my brother or, even better, marry one. To quote Mom when she first visited my lopsided railroad apartment, "Didn't I bring you up to live in a doorman building—or at least have indoor plumbing?" Well, she was wrong; I had a water closet in my living room and a bathtub in my kitchen. All indoor. But even I wonder how an introverted yeshiva girl from a family who couldn't tell a merlot from a Manischewitz survived, and eventually flourished, as a wine writer.

Survival often hinges on the back of accidents, luck, and the random kindness of strangers. When I was growing up, my salvation was losing myself in books and a whirlwind of mostly self-taught arts. My embarrassingly depressive poems were published in yearbooks. Even though I'd later hear that Isaac Bashevis Singer was actually family, being a writer seemed unobtainable, to reach for it delusional. But something strange happened when I was punching out my master's thesis (dance therapy) on the therapeutic aspects of Morris dancing. Once I began to write again, I couldn't stop. I purchased a bulky IBM Selectric. The poetry of my youth shifted to fiction, plays, and essays, and I locked myself in my apartment, battled with my inadequate spelling and worse grammar, and produced until I had the nerve to stuff pages along with that enclosed self-addressed envelope into the mailbox. My first published prose piece, in a local indie newspaper, was about a blind date and how, as nice as he was, I couldn't get past his Irish Spring soap.

Other writers warned me that should I pursue my dream, what lay in front of me was abject poverty and scathing rejection. My mother was certain that I would be forever a bum. I felt that if I didn't commit myself to what I knew I had to, I'd go through life feeling as if I had a cat clawed into my chest. There was no choice and I took my chances. I returned from my decade-long stay in Boston to New York in order to give the writing life a shot. Wine was merely one of my subjects. Food, design, and architecture were the others.

For a good decade, I was just like any other aspiring writer. My collection of short stories sat in a drawer. *Skin Burns,* a three-act, went up in tiny black-box theaters. *Home Cooking* got a reading at Manhattan Theatre Club. Nothing stuck. I looked for love. I found it. Lost it. Found it again. I creaked along. Workwise, the business section of the *New York Times* was my big fish.

Then one day I received a call from a friend.

"*Psst*, Alice," he said. "There's a guy out here in Napa who's helping wineries craft their wine so Robert Parker will give them a hundred points as a score."

I was stunned at first—how cynical was this world? Then curiosity took over—what technologies were in place to allow crafting wine to someone's taste buds? I was off to hunt the story. In 2001, for the *New York Times* biz section, I wrote that piece on technology in the wine industry, and all of a sudden I was a controversial figure. My more mainstream editors banished me as too hot to handle—they might lose advertising if they ran stories about truly artisanal wine. Napa and Big Wine's reactions? You can imagine.

I was confused. All I was doing was reporting; how was that polarizing? At the time, I didn't see myself as a whistle-blower. Yet I was in the grips of something bigger than myself. I discovered natural wine. This category was delicious, bursting with life, and made from organic grapes and none of the seventy-two-plus legal additives or with any of the technologies I had ranted about. I spent time in vineyards, I learned about viticulture and chemistry. My world exploded with travel and discovery. It was wild, energetic, and idealistic.

Like the ivory-billed woodpecker, I saw that the traditional wines of the world were endangered, and no one was saying anything about it. My more established and esteemed colleagues complained behind closed doors, but not one of them spoke up in print about the tarted-up bombastic wines that so charmed the great critic, he'd give them scores of 95 to 100 points on his subjective scale, delivering the producers to fame and fortune. Robert Parker, the Emperor of Wine, was that powerful.

How could I remain silent as well? I couldn't, and using my Word program as my sword, I wrote *The Battle for Wine and Love: Or How I Saved the World from Parkerization.* That book won me many fans and just as many enemies. There were those who applauded, but public figures remained closeted, like the prominent Bay Area wine importer who told me he couldn't give me a book blurb because Parker still reviewed the wines he sold, and he just couldn't risk it.

My book helped break the silence. Today the wine scene is completely different. The new generation has little idea who Robert Parker, Jr., is and what he meant to the wine drinkers of the world. Wine is coming back to its baseline. Natural as a category is celebrated. Organic farming is on the rise. There is no one all-powerful voice. At least when it comes to the spectrum of wine, we are living in a cornucopia period of diversity. I had plenty of time to think about all of this at the beginning of the pandemic of 2020, when many of us feared the wine shops would close.

I was quick to stock up on selections to keep the glasses full for me and my partner. But when he abandoned me to shelter at his place, where he had his toys, I found that the wines supposed to shoulder me through were failing me. In the dramatic stillness, the masked days, and the gauze-covered time, everything tasted off. Bitter, fruity, or savory, on my own with no one to clink with night after night after night that almost promised never to end, the tastes fell flat.

The essay about my experience landed in *New York* magazine. That piece wasn't about wine, though—it was about loneliness, the need for discussion and touch. Wine is the place where history, science, and civilization meet, and drinking the right glass of wine does have the power to nourish love. The essay hit a nerve and illuminated what I already knew. I write about wine because it is life.

# Author's Note

The recommendations in this book are not here because they are the best or my preferred wines but because they move me and are integral to the story line. I'm not playing favorites. In fact, some of my go-tos, my comfort zones, the Beaujolais, Bourgueil, and Chinon, the wines from the Auvergne and the southwest of France, the fabulous reds of Spain, Musar of Lebanon, some special wines from Oregon and reds from Greece, are not in this book. Maybe that's for another time. But trust me, the wines and regions I talk about here are worthy, and whether you are new to this journey or have been drinking and learning about wine for decades, all bottles and regions and wines discussed here deserve your glass.

In addition, all included fit my criteria. I drink the way I eat: organic with very little processing. They are made from at least seriously sustainable viticulture, and simply, with no added ingredients or big machines. They have either none or very little of the preservative sulfur. Some might call them natural, but these days, I just call them real.

# To Fall
# in Love,
# Drink This

# THEN THERE WAS PERFUME

I am three years old, spending the night with my mother's parents. Pop tells me a story he made up just for me, his doted-upon granddaughter. In the most creative combination of Yiddish and English, he spins some cockamamie story of these three bears who come to see the *mameleh*, who gives them a little schnapps. Once finished, he asks me, "*Mameleh*, a *bissele* schnapps?"

I reach for his comforting, papery hand, and we pad into the kitchen. Me, a wispy, sloppy redheaded toddler in Dr. Denton's. He, always meticulous, with a noble nose, whose head is never uncovered. I am fascinated by his tzitzit, the poncho-like religious undergarment with dangling fringes (he always wears it, even to bed). Seeing that the fringes are poking out from his eggplant-colored robe beneath its tie, I pull on them, almost expecting to hear a ring.

He reaches into the cupboard for the cut-glass decanter and two small glasses. He pours token amounts of whiskey for us, and he shows me how to place the glass not too close under my nose. I take an extremely short and shallow sniff. I sneeze from its heat. Pop tells me to say the *Shehakol* prayer with him, and only then am I allowed to take a sip.

Years later, on a visit, I walked into his bedroom in the afternoon. He was in that eggplant-colored robe over his suit, he

1

always wore a suit, and he had his back to me. I was amused and watched him hold the smallest of bottles to his nose. "Pop? What are you doing?" I asked him. He opened his top drawer and showed me at least a dozen more miniature perfume bottles. How completely eccentric, I thought, also charmed to discover this private fetish. This was our next training frontier; we would sniff those bottles together. For a while, we had an aroma language all our own, even if I never learned to speak adequate Yiddish or he, English. We never used descriptive words like "roses" or "peonies." We didn't need them.

My super-religious grandfather only knew of philosophers like Maimonides, but I would have loved to throw Immanuel Kant's notion to him that smell was the "most ungrateful" and "most dispensable" of the senses. Perhaps Pop would have snapped back that that *meshugana* German philosopher was wrong, because according to the *Zohar,* the Jewish mystical interpretation of the Bible, the sense of smell reaches even a higher plane than wisdom and understanding. Maybe that was what Pop was trying to do with me, sharpen my instincts to know what was right and what was wrong. And yes, show me how something so simple could bring so much pleasure.

Pop's sensory training didn't stop with perfume, booze, or *Shabbos*'s sticky-sweet wine. When Pop tapped out basil-seed-size Sen-Sen, that intense licorice candy, he would make me smell it first. During the after-*Shabbos* ritual called *havdalah*, he held the spice box crammed with cinnamon, clove, and allspice under my nose longer than anyone else's. Then, of course, there was the perfume.

Born in 1888, Pop didn't arrive from Europe to America until 1919. By the time I entered the picture, he was sixty-six, and he always looked ancient. He had white hair and beard, and his nerdy black horn-rimmed glasses sat on his proud, chiseled, sensitive nose. When he draped his striped prayer shawl over his head and rocked in meditation, he not only looked Old Testament, he acted it. If I mispronounced a Hebrew word, he'd poke me in the arm. If I plunked out the wrong note on the piano when he asked me to accompany his singing, he scolded me. I don't know what it was, maybe the smell of his unconditional love, that didn't change when he was impatient. I didn't mind even when he took me to the chicken slaughterhouse where he worked as a *shoichet,* killing birds according to the kosher laws, severing the trachea, esophagus, carotid arteries, jugular veins, and vagus nerve, with his decisive executioner's speed. He never let me see his technique in action, but I did watch him sharpen his knives to obsessive-compulsive precision. Even now, I can't ever look at a chicken, no matter how fancy its preparation, without synesthetically smelling the air that was around me—dank, dark blood on sawdust. Nevertheless, it's a fond memory.

While no one in my family ever would dare to snicker when Pop raised a soup spoon to his nose before eating, I was continually ridiculed—that is, until my parents and my brother and I were driving south for a rare family vacation in Miami. Where accents turned twangy, we pulled off the road for the night. In a diner near our motel, we sat shoulder to shoulder in a red vinyl booth. Mom pulled up the menu and looked at the options. "There's exactly one item here that is kosher. Just one." She was annoyed that the world wasn't a Jewish bubble.

The waitress placed our orders in front of us. Four starched trout arrived, broiled on "tinfoil," as Mom had requested, so that no *traif* pig or shellfish would touch our food.

I was nine years old, and the only fish I knew intimately were Mrs. Paul's frozen sticks, pickled herring, and Grandma's gefilte fish. When that broiled creature was laid down in front of me, eyes looking in my direction, I looked back at it, trying to figure it out. I pulled away my long red braid so it wouldn't fall into the dish. I lowered my nose.

"Here she goes. She's starting," my mother said, shaking her head.

I pushed the plate away, wrinkling my nose in disgust. And while I went to bed hungry, I was the only one that night not heaving into the toilet. Until that moment, I smelled for pleasure. The fish incident taught me that there were other uses, danger being one of them. Later I would find out that falling in love was another. If a man smelled like truffles to me, I was helpless. Hey, I thought, if a dog could smell the past, present, and future, why couldn't I?

On my twenty-first birthday, my grandfather knocked on my bedroom door. I was on summer break from college, and we were at my mother's house in Baldwin, Long Island. He adjusted his large black *kippah* and said in his fractured English, "*Mameleh.*" He took a breath and looked at me and stroked my hair. "A girl is like a flower." An imaginary daisy appeared between his two fingers. "For a minute, she is beautiful and firm." he waved his hand. "Everyone wants to hold her. Everyone wants to smell her. Just as she's enjoying the attention the most"—he pulled fantasy petals off one by one and shook his head—"it's time to find a husband."

I ran to tell my mother, laughing because I felt that nothing could affect his adoration of me. "Pop is telling me that my petals are falling." Deceived by trust, seduced by the adventure of youth, I didn't realize that I was smelling something that would unravel.

When I was in Boston for graduate school, my love of odors led me to explore the world of taste and wine. I kept my first love, Stephen, a lawyer and a Catholic, hidden from my mother and grandfather. But Pop must have sniffed that something was not kosher. One evening, I picked up the phone.

"Alice Feiring?" asked a man with a heavy Brooklyn accent. Confused, I answered, "Yes."

"Your grandfather, Shmiel, gave me your phone number. We go to the same *shul.*" He went on to tell me that he worked at the post office and studied Talmud at night. My grandfather had told him I was pretty and single. No, he never read any literature, not even I. B. Singer. And yes, I intended to work and not stay home and have children. Yet, even though I was in graduate school, not looked upon kindly in that world of ultraorthodox Jewery, just being Reb Shmiel's granddaughter made me desirable.

Would I come down to New York to have coffee or tea somewhere? I had nothing against a postal worker, though a Bukowski-like genius (okay, one who wasn't a drunkard) would have been more aligned with my dreams. But I grasped for an excuse. I had exams. I didn't think I could. I was so very sorry.

"*Vat es* this, 'in common'? He is man. You are a lady. He has a *zeh gut* job." Pop was not only furious but took it as an affront. My refusal was an embarrassment. Nothing was worse to him than that. He had grown impatient nine years after the flower tête-à-tête and believed my petals were oxidized and smelling of rot, like that trout. Being the *Mameleh* didn't protect me from my bad behavior.

He could be so stubborn, as I understood his mother had been as well. She, after whom I was named, was a shtetl firecracker. In the 1870s when she was seventeen, her father came home and said, "*Mazel tov,* you're going to be a bride."

She told her father if he forced her to marry a man whom she didn't love, she'd never speak to him again. She made good on her threat.

My grandfather and his sister, Feigle (Fanny), was born of that unhappy marriage. Four years from Pop's birth, in a tiny shtetl outside of Lvov, his mother managed to get herself a divorce, remarry, and emigrate to the United States with her new husband, their infant, and Fanny, leaving Pop behind. I heard that he would cry to my grandmother about his early abandonment, but he inherited his mother's unblinking will and facile harshness. From whom, I wondered, came his appreciation of the sensual sense of smell?

I never did call the postman, but I did return to New York City, proceeding to smell every wine that came my way.

Sometime after Pop's hundredth birthday, he slowed down. I'd visit, walking into his cluttered apartment, and there would be the flinty, dark, and bitterly sweet scent of freshly sharpened pencils. My God, there were hundreds of them stuffed in empty pickle jars with obsessively whittled points. I'd open windows to air out the smells and the dust, run errands, sit with him. Over some weeks I began to realize the conversation was one-sided. I invented excuses, "Oh, he's deaf," but I knew he heard when he wanted to. I tried to ignore how he stopped taking my head in his hands and kissing its crown.

There was one particular day when I registered what I did not want to believe. I left in tears, and as I shut the door, I heard his nurse, Freda, plead with him in Yiddish: *"Redn tsu ir! Zi iz di mameleh!"* Speak to her. She is the *mameleh*.

On the Friday of Labor Day weekend, he was admitted to a Brooklyn hospital with a sharp pain in his belly. I sat with my mother for hours. "You go home," my mother said to me.

It was getting close to *Shabbos,* not an issue for me, but my mother was eager to get me out of there before sunset. I took Pop's still warm hand and kissed his cheek, leaving my mother by his bedside. An hour and a half later as I entered my apartment, the phone rang. My mother was back in her Long Beach apartment. She heaved a sigh and said tearlessly, "He asked me what time it was. Then he told me he had enough. And that was it. The end. He died." He was nearly 104.

Perhaps my mother was truly as unaffected by his death as she sounded, but her father loomed over her life, she was alone, and that was wrong. I grabbed a toothbrush and hopped on the train to Long Island. That night I slept in the mahogany bed that had been my grandfather's, from so long ago, the same one that we sat on while uncapping perfume bottles. As I was closing my eyes, I smelled him, although he hadn't slept in it for years.

If I'd had to describe how Pop smelled to me back when I was a child, I might have said nothing more than old. Even though his smell was very specific, that would have been the extent of my descriptive ability. But when I'm assessing an aged wine, like from Rioja, or something antique and amber from the country of Georgia, and describe its aroma and taste—parchment, dust, spice box with cloves, a combined savory herbal scent of history and connection—I know I am describing the way my grandfather smelled to me when I was young and my hand knew no better place than in his. When I use those words to describe wines I'm inextricably pulled to, I'm sensing Pop. These are words saved for certain kinds of wine that seem to come from an old world that no longer exists, and yet I mourn them. These are aromas and tastes from the past that take me back to a time of unconditional love that I trusted would never end.

# DRINK THIS

Wine: Mingaco Vino Blanco
Grape: Moscatel de Alejandria
Where: Itata Valley, Chile

Despite a certain smoky topaz color, this wine felt so fresh and bright with lemon and the barest touch of bitter. Some scents were floral, some were malodorous. Some were other-worldly, with threads of dusty, bitter, savory, and often there was that ancient something compelling me to take more sips. The sensations kept on coming. But there was always that orange rind, which tapped down what could have been explosive perfume but transformed the taste into "digestible"; it felt good in my body. The lack of pomp and circumstance and the aromatic simplicity and power of that wine with scratch and honeysuckle went to my head, making me remember that, from the beginning, aromatic wines spoke to me.

When I asked a friend in Germany who tracks the wine market, "Are perfumy wines still out of favor?" she had a quick retort, "I don't know, but I can tell you this—I gag when I smell them."

I burst out laughing. She and I have drunk so many wines together, and many of them have been absolutely of the aromatic type. I swear I've seen her like them. But she is not alone in a knee-jerk reaction of *blech*. There are reasons people deride wines that smell like an exotic flower shop left without air-conditioning for too long or, as she would say, flat-bubble bathwater, and she's not wrong. So many of them are just a little too tough to love, but I think of them as a delightful underdog appealingly wagging its tail for attention.

If only I could put one—an amber-colored wine, fully yummy—in front of her, she'd change her mind. Anyone would. The Mingaco is a delicious wine, made by children of nature, Pablo Pedreros and Daniela de Pablo Mendoza, from the most aromatic grape of them all, muscat.

Muscat is the cliché aromatic grape. Put your nose in it, and the honeysuckle is crazy identifiable, kind of profound. The grape's name tracks back two thousand years, and there are colorful theories to its etymology. One of the best is that it was named for the fragrance derived from the gland of the male musk deer. The grape, which grows worldwide, flourished in the Mediterranean and has two hundred distinct variations from white, pinkish, or black-berried varieties. Fun fact: Muscat d'Alexandria was reputed to have been the base of Queen Cleopatra's favorite wines. To experience what the queen might have savored, select a wine made the way it was during her reign, fermented on the skin, like red wine, for three weeks or longer. This technique, called "skin contact," often makes an amber-colored wine. The skin lends texture and color and tamps down intense aromas into a complexity that fires up the senses and, for me, gives those kinds of old-fashioned subtleties I love. That was the way the Mingaco was made.

Muscat, moscatel (or zibibbo as it is called in Sicily), or whatever you want to call it, came over to Chile when the 1554 Spanish conquistadors brought grapevines to South America. Today, especially in the south of Chile, Bío Bío, Maule, and Itata—sturdy, fat old vines are still healthy and able to produce grapes. These have survived for up to three centuries, having witnessed revolutions and dictators. When their fruit is made into wine using that skin-contact tradition, magic happens. This technique hung on long after Cleopatra, especially in peasant culture, mutes the aromatic, gives a raspy texture, and especially when made naturally, the extra tannin protects the wine from degradation. The resulting wines can be a pleasure to smell, and the texture turns the wine into an eloquent food partner.

Yet merely the grape's name, muscat, can trigger grimaces, most likely because moscatel was the preferred drink of Depression-era Bowery drunks—MD20/20, made by Mogen David but nicknamed Mad Dog, the definition of plonk. That concoction was made from some manner of muscat grape fortified with grain alcohol, then brown-bagged and chugged for a cheap buzz. So, there's the snobbery. Who wants to like plonk? Other critics brace themselves, expecting that aromatic wines will taste as perfumy as they smell. Others associate them with the fizz, Moscato d'Asti, of which I admit there's about one worthy of drinking (Vittorio Bera et Figli). Others complain that wines from aromatic grapes are flabby, without "energy," because they are by nature not high-acid grapes. I admit, there are many boring, one-note wines out there. Yet the good ones always spoke to me. I know why. It all goes back to my grandfather.

But I wasn't thinking of Pop when I was dusty from the broken Chilean roads to Chekura. I can't imagine what he would have made of the village that used to be a wine and wheat basket in the region of Itata, about a six-hour drive south of Santiago. Chile—hot, dry, wild—would have been foreign to him, but he would have loved to put his powerful nose in those wines.

Pedro and Daniela led me up their weird steps, made of old buried tires, to the traditional adobe home they were building with their bare hands. Daniela cooed at the baby strapped to her chest. Hospitable vegans, they put out spectacular home-made chips and crisps. I kept thinking of Friulian winemaker Josko Gravner's quote, "To make a natural wine, you must be a natural person." These folk? They were über-natural.

Once we climbed up to the dwelling in progress, we stood on the peak overlooking the valley, and Pablo explained that the name of their village, Chekura, referred to the way the villagers practiced collective harvest: One's problems and joys were also their neighbors'. They helped each other.

Their new wine had just been poured, a pipeño blanco. While a *pipeño* is a barrel made of the local beechwood (*raulí*), it also refers to a Chilean farmer's wine of any color. Drinking it on that spendidly clear day, the wine stimulated my brain's wild button. One sip and I was hanging out in the Forum with Plato. Another pulled me next to Beethoven as he scribbled down the score for his cello sonata No. 3 in A major. The next breath and I was ducking out of the way as a priest swung his censer, filling the air with smoky spice. Even now, give me a Mingaco and the visions prance, bringing me back to a couple at the beginning of their voyage and desires.

## DRINK THESE AROMATIC WINES

Chile isn't the only hot spot for these wines, and muscat (and its variations) isn't the only fragrant variety. Greece is a home base for other aromatic rarities like santameriana and chlori. Again with a bit of skin contact, you get an amber wine that is bound to stimulate your imagination. These are also often ageable, and become waxy and more subtle but no less exciting with time.

Rivera del Notro
Wine: Blanco
Grape: Muscat (with Corinto and Sémillon)
Where: Itata Valley, Chile

Cacique Maravilla
Wine: Vino Naranja
Grape: Moscatel de Alejandria
Where: Yumbel, Chile

Viña González Bastías
Wine: Naranjo
Grape: Pink Muscat, Torrontel, País
Where: Maule Valley, Chile

De Martino
Wine: Viejas Tinajas
Grape: Muscat
Where: Itata Valley, Chile

Sant'Or
Wine: Santameriana
Grape: Santameriana
Where: Peloponnese, Greece

Terra
Wine: Ambera Deep Skin
Grape: Muscat d'Alexandria
Where: Lemnos, Greece

Papras Bio Wines
Wine: Ore-ads
Grape: Black Muscat of Tyrnavos
Where: Tyrnavos, Mount Olympus, Greece

Siflogo
Wine: Chlori
Grape: Chlori
Where: Lefkada, Greece

Mortellito
Wine: Viaria Bianco
Grape: Moscato di Noto
Where: Noto, Sicily, Italy

Tanca Nica
Wine: Ghirbí
Grape: Zibibbo
Where: Pantelleria, Sicily, Italy

Nino Barraco
Wine: Zibibbo
Grape: Zibibbo
Where: Marsala, Sicily, Italy

Domaine Matassa
Wine: Cuvée Alexandria
Grape: Muscat d'Alexandria
Where: Roussillon, France

# PHOTO SESSION

With freshly tightened braces, I met my father at his New York City law office. We were going to take the train back to Long Island. Leaning on his doorjamb, I watched as he talked on the phone, his back to me, waving his hand about like a conductor in a slow movement. Before he hung up, I could have sworn he whispered "I love you" to whoever was on the other line. And yes, I could guess.

"Hey, Dad," I said.

He spun around, big smile on his face, and stroked that new goatee of his. "What do you say about going to Saint Marks Place?"

"Now?" I looked up to his clock. "Do we have time?" Sundown would be in about five hours, and my mother always was furious if we cut it too close.

"Plenty," he said. "We can catch the three-thirty."

Turns out that my philandering dad needed an expensive haircut.

In those months before Woodstock, I was a barely pubescent, painfully shy yeshiva girl who couldn't smile without covering my mouth with my hand. However, in my daydreams, I was powerful, sassy. I longed to drop acid, talk philosophy, and trail Dylan. To someone like me, trapped out on Long Island, speaking Hebrew for half the day, feeling stifled and longing to be at least nineteen, the East Village was paradise. Obviously, I didn't say no. We arrived in a taxi. We walked into Paul McGregor's salon, and what a surprise, Phyllis was there waiting. Miniskirt, high boots, close-cropped Twiggy cut. She tried to kiss me. I backed away. "Are you going to get your hair cut too?" she asked me, pulling on my red frizz.

"No. I'm headed to the bookstore across the street."

Dad said sure and pulled out a five-dollar bill for me. "Knock yourself out. Be back in an hour."

Free. I was free in 1969's psychedelic spring. Once inside the East Side Bookstore, I approached the cash register and asked the pale man in a tie-dyed T-shirt with a ponytail to his waist, "Where would I find Camus?"

"Up the stairs. Existentialists are all near the window."

It was empty there, and the smell of books reminded me of leaves in an autumnal forest. I found what I was looking for and had pulled *The Plague* off a shelf when I felt a breath on the top of my head.

"Camus?" a man's voice asked.

I spun around and saw a tall man with long bones, black hair in tight waves, with a strong, square jaw. Behind John Lennon wire glasses, his eyes were two unblinking beads. I suppose he was handsome. He was tall, very skinny, but those eyes, almost cross-eyed, freaked me out. I didn't like him.

I whispered, "'Scuse me."

I wanted to stay in that bookstore longer but, intimidated, I tiptoed down to the register to pay. However, as soon as I was out the door, he was behind me. "Trying to get away?" he asked.

Busted, I thought, and had no idea how to break away without exposing my mistrust, that I'd judged him before knowing him, on instinct. The trouble with him knowing was that it was 1969; I was supposed to love and believe everyone. Lacking a proper excuse—"no" didn't seem like it would work—I told him I had only a short while and agreed to walk on Second Avenue, just for a bit. I knew that part of town well, as I was often at Rapoport's Dairy restaurant with my parents. Stars from the nearby Yiddish theater were always hanging out, dipping their hands in the bowls of dusty dried chickpeas, *arbes*, on the table. And then at the next table there could be Jimi Hendrix doing the same thing, a sight that you'd never see in some dull kosher deli on Long Island. As we neared that corner, he told me his name, Jon Berger. Hearing a Jewish name made me feel more at ease. In fact, I chided myself for thinking ill of a fellow Jew. He told me a little about himself: He had come from California to study film and photography at NYU. He was Roman Polanski's student. I had recently seen *Rosemary's Baby*, and it gave me nightmares for weeks. Polanski was married to the actress Sharon Tate, and they were expecting. Just a few months later, the actress and the unborn would be murdered by the Manson Family in Los Angeles.

Impressed, I asked, "What's he like?"

"Nice," he said, "we hang out a lot. Smart guy."

I imagined he had to have genuine talent to get into that class, or maybe they let him in because he was older, twenty-four, like Peter, the boy on my block I'd had a crush on since I had been a little girl.

We reached the corner of Sixth Street, where the Fillmore sat. He announced, "This is my block," and surprised me by adding, "I'd love to photograph you."

I might have been in ninth grade, but that didn't make

me an idiot. After all, I knew about human behavior from reading the advice columnist Ann Landers and reading, well, Camus. What was more, I believed myself to be homely. I had wispy hair and braces, for God's sake. Flattery made me suspicious.

He must have felt my fears because he clarified, "Your colors are intense. Your red fluffy hair, those red snaps on that shiny black raincoat, the day's fog? You'd be more of a painting than a photograph. If you could look at yourself as I do, you'd see what I mean."

This wasn't the first time an artist had wanted me to model. I used to sit for a woman in town who loved my "peachy" complexion. My dad took photographs all the time. Mr. Finkelstein, the photojournalist who lived behind us, often asked me to pose. While I might have thought my interior life a dark place, my exterior was colorful.

"It's important for people to be trustworthy, to be sincere," he said in a way that seemed insincere to me.

I thought about this. He was right. We had to believe in people. On the other hand, was I obligated to like this guy?

"You're perfectly safe with me."

"People often mean exactly the opposite of what they say," I said reflexively.

"You're too young to be this cynical."

I was most certainly not too young. Since I'd turned fourteen, almost everything I counted on had been ripped away, I'd felt myself age. I thought nothing worse could happen, so I agreed, even as I knew I was being bullied. "Fine. It must be quick. My father's waiting for me."

"Your father?" he asked.

"My father."

"Twenty minutes will be plenty of time." He was pleased.

His building was a three-floor town house adjacent to the Odyssey House, a drug rehab. I noticed a shul nearby too. I felt almost protected. He headed to the stairs to his building. I stayed at the iron gate. He turned around to me. "Aren't you coming?"

"No," I said, my fingers holding the iron gate from the roadside. "I'm not going inside. We can shoot out here."

He gave me this look, as if saying, *Again*?

But I wasn't budging. "I'm not going into your apartment. Out here is perfectly fine." I felt exhausted from the effort of standing up for myself.

"Fine. We can go to the roof, then."

I thought, Okay, if necessary, I could scream.

The hallway was painted a sickly mint green. The stairs were lopsided with age. I waited outside his apartment and then followed him up to the roof. The air was humid and misty, and the trees were still bare but had fat buds like bullets. "Wow," I said. "It's so great up here." I ran to the edge to look down at buildings. It felt so, well, urban. Exotic. New York at its finest.

With him he had a flash, a tripod, a Polaroid, and a thirty-five-millimeter. I don't know what it was, but it wasn't a Nikon.

"You walk like a ballerina; you dance?" he asked me while setting up.

I told him yes.

"Take off your raincoat," he ordered.

"What happened to the colors?" I asked, remembering how he'd gotten me up there in the first place.

He looked annoyed. I left my shiny slicker on. Resigned, he snapped away.

"Where is your father?" he asked.

"Paul McGregor's. Getting his hair cut while his girlfriend looks on."

"His girlfriend?"

"He's having an affair."

"My father fucked around too," he said. "Does your mother know?"

"No."

"Hold still. Look at me."

I was much more comfortable looking away, off to the distance. I turned my face to him and tried as best as I could to cover my braces and keep my mouth shut.

"Now move. Show me what you can do." He pointed his camera.

I started out slowly, warming up with some tap dancing, a bit of a shuffle-off-to-Buffalo. Then the performer in me took over. I leaped, spun, and twirled in the mist, almost working into a frenzy, dancing out everything that was going in my life. In the span of only a few months, I saw that my father's affair with Phyllis had accelerated. My brother had been on his deathbed with viral pneumonia, then he'd deserted me for college. On the day before Succoth my grandmother rolled and pinched *kreplach* for the holiday meal. What seemed like common word loss in the afternoon morphed into a massive stroke by the evening. Half her body was paralyzed, and so was her speech center. She did not die soon enough for her wishes, and my mother was burdened with her care. Both of my father's parents had died, one from cancer, one by slipping in the too-hot tub. (When my mother returned to the car after identifying the body—lucky her—she told me, "She looked like a boiled chicken.") Becky had died. Becky, the dog of my youth, my protector.

I was alone.

And there I was, dancing for a weird stranger on a rooftop. Five minutes into my improvisation of despair, I heard a crack of thunder. I stopped, shocked. There were a few drops. Then we were being pelted.

"Help me!" he yelled, his face twisted up like a mad scientist's. I obeyed as he shoved his tripod in my arm. I followed him down the steps and hesitated before going into the apartment, teetering on the cusp of fear and fascination. I crossed the threshold.

In a claustrophobic hallway, a telephone table stood to my left, but no telephone. A corkboard hung above it. A closet-size kitchen was directly at the other end of the entrance. The bathroom was off to the right, and to the left was a living room that faced Sixth Street and was a student-like mess with cinder blocks propping up shelves that had no books. There was no furniture, not even a chair. There were a few pillows, lighting equipment, cameras, and lots of women's clothing strewn about, in piles and on the floor, as if hastily discarded. The whole scene looked temporary. Even my brother's dorm room was more done up. I could swear I smelled ghosts.

He reached into a closet and pulled out a bright, floral, silky kimono. "Want to change?" he asked me, with a bit of a smirk, so I couldn't tell if he was serious or not. I laughed. He had to be joking, chiding me for my caution. Yet I clutched the Camus, holding it as a shield. "I really have to go," I said.

"Just wait one second," he said. "I want you to see the kind of work I do. I'm a real photographer. Take a look." He handed me a thick stack of Polaroids, saying, "I'll be right back," and slipped into the nearby toilet. Did he go inside to pee or to shoot up speed or maybe even heroin? While listening for telling sounds, not that I would know what those were, I put down my book to better eye the images in my hand. Unbeknownst to my mom, my father slid *Playboys* in between the comic books in "the kids bathroom," but the images this stranger had given me were nothing like those. These were women with women. Women with men. Some were alone. Those were the ones that made me gasp. Naked and posed. Some seemed lifeless. I didn't know what I was looking at. Everything inside of me screamed, *Get out.*

The door was locked.

A dark metal pole like some medieval contraption angled from the lock to the floor. I pushed. I swirled. I poked. I had no idea what it was or how to manipulate it. The door wouldn't budge. It looked impossible to open. I didn't know where the catch was or if there even was a catch. I sensed that I didn't have the luxury of time. I heard the bathroom door creak open.

I turned around. He had a large smile on his face. Without looking at him directly, I could tell, it was unmistakable—he was naked from the waist down. His was the first erection I had ever seen. Pointed at me, it was a menacing weapon. "You're not leaving," he said to me.

*Let me out of here* rang between my ears but not out of my mouth. I was resolute. No way in hell would I show him I was scared. Absolutely not. Fuck him. I was not. The fear was choking me, and the tears were building up. But I knew without a doubt that I could not show any vulnerability. Guided by some spirit or wizardry or dumb luck, because I can't figure out any other way it happened, I managed to pry the door open as he tried to grab me. I skidded down the stairs. Hitting the second landing, I realized, dunce that I was, I'd forgotten to grab my paperback, and in a moment of epic stupidity, I reversed course and pounded on his door as I shouted, "Book, please!"

I heard him approach and he opened the door, his pants back on. I sprang back to the steps so he couldn't drag me into his apartment. Yet I noticed he looked completely different, almost normal, the intent on his face gone. He had turned into a garden snake from a viper. Like a timid stranger, he held out *The Plague.* I snatched it out of those long fingers of his, and I scrambled down the steps once more, Camus in my fist as he pleaded after me, "I won't hurt you. Just let me masturbate!"

"Yeah, right!" I finally screamed back at him. "And thanks for being sincere!" I was so angry that he had tricked me.

Darting between the raindrops, I reached my newly coiffed father, waiting and not looking at all concerned. On the train to Baldwin, my dad pretended he hadn't had a hookup, and I pretended I hadn't been a fool. As he read his *New York Law Journal,* I had my nose in *The Plague,* not reading but reliving every moment. Dad turned to me. "You okay?"

"Why?" I said nonchalantly. "I'm fine."

I was not. I was furious with myself. Why didn't I listen to my initial mistrust for that Jon Berger? Ah well, I thought, no real harm done. My heart, beating like a hummingbird's, knew differently.

My mother had just made it back from Brooklyn, and already her *Shabbos* dinner was perfuming the house. The chicken soup smells were like Valium. "Hi, Mom," I yelled, then I raced up to my parents' bedroom, the only place where I could close the door and make a private call. I flopped down on their round bed and called my brother, a freshman at Stony Brook. "Andy! My God. I'm so glad you are there," I whispered into the phone.

"What's the matter?" he asked.

"Nothing. Look, I have an idea, so don't think I'm a complete dumbass, but what exactly does a guy do when he masturbates?"

"Shit. What happened?"

"Just tell me, please. *Shabbos* is any second."

In his pre-med fashion, he explained the mechanics of ejaculation.

"Okay, he wasn't going to rape me, he was just a pervert," I discerned, getting the picture.

"Mouse, what happened?"

My mother called up to me with urgency, "Alice! *Shabbos!* I'm lighting the candles. Get off the phone!"

"Come on," Andrew pushed me.

I got the story out as quickly as I could, not skipping over Phyllis. My brother had never listened to me so intently. "Wait," I said, and immediately hushed myself. Someone had picked up the kitchen line. "Alice, get off."

"I'm talking to Andrew."

"Hi, Mom," he said.

"*Tateleh.*" I could hear her light right up. "Have a good *Shabbos.*"

"Two minutes, okay? Please?" I asked. There was silence, but I didn't trust it. "Mom, hang up. Please."

Finally, we heard the click. Andrew just kept on saying,

"I can't believe it. I can't believe it. You're smarter than that."

"It was okay," I said.

"No, it was not okay. He could have been a serial killer. Do you get it?"

"Honestly, he was just a pervert," I said, my heart starting to go staccato. "If he was a killer, I would have known."

"And knowing you, you'd be too scared you'd hurt his feelings, and instead of saying take a hike, well, you'd go along with it until he twisted your neck."

"Stop."

"You cannot be worried about other people's feelings, especially maniacs. Do you get it? You knew he was bad news. And still you were scared to let him know you didn't trust him. Is this a girl thing? You are so lucky. Look, Al, whatever you do," he said, "don't tell Mom."

As if I was ever going to let her know about this one. My mother lived in fear of everything. If she knew the whole story, she'd lock me in the basement forever. In an hour, maybe, *Shabbos* wine would make my heart slow down. That sweet stuff would never taste as good to me. I went downstairs just as she was waving her hands over the candles. I watched as she put her hands over her eyes. I could imagine what she was praying for. My father was nowhere in sight.

## DRINK THIS

Bénédicte et Stéphane Tissot
Singulier
Grape: Trousseau
Where: Arbois, Jura, France

This wine seemed like a charming innocent who went off to the Sorbonne, smoked fiendishly, danced with frenzy, and yet could perform a flawless pirouette, and so clever, getting rid of bat guano or rewiring an old house is just in a day's work. The wine had me at its energy, and then it finished me off with its sensuality. Oh the aroma, full of something like a fancy talcum powder with crushed rose petals. All of this in a sublime, medium, silky body sporting the kind of acidity that can match with gefilte fish. Thank you.

Like many of her generation, my mother, Ethel, born in 1924, never outgrew her taste for clichéd kosher wines. Was it just her madeleine or did she just not know better? Manischewitz or Carmel or Schapiro's, it didn't matter which one, all those sweet koshers tasted like liquefied grape jelly. Whatever. Ever since I was in diapers, I drank them every Friday night, Saturday afternoon, and holidays. Of course, at the beginning, my parents mixed my tipple with seltzer. By the time I was seven or so, full strength. That stuff was mother's milk to me, I confess. So in the aftermath of my escape from Jon Berger's apartment at fourteen, I ran down for *Shabbos* dinner and gratefully sucked it down.

I was even more thankful when, years later, I found another wine world, made from organic agriculture and one ingredient, grape. So different than the conventional wines that were made to a market with all the technology available to the industry. These natural ones were the only ones worth my liver. This was not about ideology over aesthetic; they tasted better, the way a fresh-picked heirloom tomato tastes more complex than anything you can get in a package in the supermarket. Through sipping, those delicious wines also told stories of the people and year that made them. To me, these were way more kosher than anything with a certification. Because, except for one impossible-to-find kosher wine from Australia (Harkham), kosher and natural rarely existed. Depending on how you count, there are seventy-two perfectly legal wine additives (available in kosher, of course), and for the sweet wine my mother drank? Were those made from grape concentrate instead of real fruit? Most likely. Yet even the top Catholic brass, Pope Francis, agreed with me when he declared that only wines without additives were holy enough for the Eucharist. So why not for my fellow Jews?

This was one of my first-world problems. I couldn't drink the old slop or what passed for modern kosher wines. What was I going to do while sharing a holiday with my mother when drinking was required not only for my mental health but for custom, like at Passover? Which led to the fifth question of the Passover celebration: Why on that night was I unable to find any natural kosher wines?

Ethel—who chose religion over just about everything else, never lost her thrill for going to temple, dressing in a smart suit with a favorite diamond bug pin on her lapel ("Have to advertise," she'd say), sitting in the women's section—could never quite grasp my desperation to find something palatable to drink. My desire to have a glass with a meal was almost unseemly to her. "There's a big jug of Matuk in the fridge, and it's delicious," she'd say, unable to believe this obsessed redhead was really her daughter. Invariably for holidays, I'd plunk down way too much money, hopes high, expectations low, ferrying the rabbi-approved bottles over to Mom's apartment in Long Beach, where, as the family shrank and shriveled, we celebrated, if you could call it that, at a table for two. To her credit, she'd always taste, yet would say, "You know what this needs?" then she'd mix some of her favorite, Matuk Rouge Soft, with the thirty-five-dollar (kosher) Burgundy I'd brought, and then she'd nod. "That's better." Which really didn't matter because that Burgundy sucked anyway.

That's why one year I got it into my head to make my own: traditional, kosher, and natural. Of course, I couldn't *make* it. As an *apikores,* nonbeliever, I couldn't touch the grapes, tread, or punch them down. I was, however, allowed to look at them. You see, kosher wine doesn't mean it was blessed by a rabbi, it means that it was made by a Shabbos-observing Jew. And if it didn't go through the draconic process of being flash-pasteurized, only an observant Jew could open the bottle and serve it to another observant Jew. Ironically, my mother, who doesn't even turn on a light between Friday sunset and Saturday sundown, could be a kosher winemaker and sommelier. Me? Not a chance. However, I could be my own consultant and find a Sabbath observer to do the physical handling. I felt I had to do it, not just for my own pleasure but for my people who didn't have a clue what real wine was like.

I set out to make my wine in the country of Georgia. I loved the wines. I knew I could get affordable grapes and had friends to help out, even a Sabbath-observing one. All I had to do was figure out how to pay for the kosher certification, which could be as much as ten thousand dollars, and deal with the bureaucracy, like finding the rabbi to give certification. It wasn't easy to reach the man in Tbilisi. The rabbi was always rushing out to Kutaisi for a bris or to Baghdati for a wedding. Finally, I trapped him over Skype. After the Jew-splaining treatise on the religious laws and why I, now a secular Jewish natural-wine lover, would never make my wine, we were disconnected. I called back. Friends in Tbilisi tried to reach him. The harvest came and went. It was clear that I wasn't going to be making kosher wine that vintage, but I had made up my mind: I wasn't going to endure bad wine for the holiday any longer.

On the occasion of the second Passover of the pandemic, I'd had enough suffering. I had long ago become a full adult, and it was time for my own liberation. I headed to Discovery Wines and tried to find the wine that would serve me with pleasure on the night when you were supposed to drink four cups. There on the shelf, it called out to me. Bénédict and Stéphane Tissot's Singulier.

The Tissots are an hour's drive east from Burgundy or a forty-five-minute ride from Dijon. I loved the wines from that region, and when I first visited, I knew why: The place itself was soothing with its rolling hills and Irish-like greenery, cows marching through the vines with their bells donging, as if telling me to slow down and park all anxiety. I'm a sucker for morel mushrooms, which are plentiful here, likewise Comté cheese. But the Jura also has a spirit of rebellion, an independent streak, and was a sweet spot for the resistance fighters in World War II. There was peace and sparkling air, and the wines had an originality, a lack of cynicism, and a lack of commercialism. Physically, it's the mirror image of Burgundy, but the wines are fresher. Their most famous wine, and most expensive, is Vin Jaune, a wine made like an unfortified sherry—meaning it develops a yeast veil called "flor" that protects the wine as it loses its fruit and intensifies over the years until it's bottled. It can be sublime and tastes like an unsweet salted caramel. There are other versions of wine made from the same grape, savagnin (often mistaken for sauvignon), and can be made in the same salty style, but when not aged for a shorter time, it tastes like a boat ride out in the ocean spray. Chardonnay drinkers? This might be the place for my favorite expressions where the wine feels like silvery water. Nothing buttery here. The Jura also grows brilliant pinot noir, but its special power is in the other red grapes, the ethereal poulsard and the grippier trousseau. Compared to Burgundy, all of their reds are light in weight. Each one has a different poem to parse. The Singulier. Forty bucks. I hesitated. That was more than I usually spent on my singular drinking pleasure. Damn it, I thought, I'm worth it.

Back at home, I took out a favorite calligraphy marker, sat

down at my kitchen table, and got to work. Like a tattoo art-ist, I found my spot. On the Tissot label, I carefully drew a U inside of an O, with a KP alongside, the symbol for "Union of Orthodox Rabbis, Kosher for Passover." It was official. With the help of a little forgery, I'd made my first kosher wine.

It's not that I was trying to hoodwink my mother—it's not like I was bringing a loaf of rye into a house that was a matzo zone or tricking her to eat *traif* shrimp while tell-ing her it was flounder. She tasted my unkosher wines every other time of the year, but somehow on Passover, she looked for that "Kosher for Passover" mark on everything, including instant coffee. That wine was as kosher (and as kosher for Passover) as eating an apple from the tree. I'd had it with the sixteenth-century rabbis who argued in and wrote the Tal-mud's problematic interpretation of what kosher wine was. My wine was kosher in spirit and in ingredients. On top of it, my handiwork looked damned good.

That night at our seder for two, the candles lit and the Haggadahs out, I poured the first glass into my grandfather's silver cup. That was absolutely the most gorgeous kosher wine I ever had. I was enjoying the seder, not counting the hours until it was over and we could sing "Chad Gadya."

"Taste?" I asked Ethel as she was watching my rapture with laughter. She raised an eyebrow and picked the bottle up, not even looking for the kosher symbol.

Do we ever outgrow our desire for a parent's understand-ing and approval? Even if we have another decade left, my mother will never quite accept my rejection of religion. But if she understood why I've devoted decades to writing about this magical, enduring symbol of life, culture, and humanity without shaking her head and saying, "Give it up already," that would suit me even better.

Mom was fragile that year. COVID had pitted her memory and fueled her anxiety reactions. Yet as she poured some wine gamely into her own silver goblet, she crinkled her nose. "Not bad," she said, and my heart perked up. Maybe she would understand. But then she picked up the Matuk Rouge Soft (naturally sweetened, of course) and blended it with Tissot's trousseau. She was satisfied. "Taste it," she insisted, pushing the goblet in my direction.

## DRINK THESE JURASSIC WINES

You can almost never go wrong with a Jurassic producer. Many of them are so, so good. Most are made in small quantities normally, but with recent bouts of hail and early frost and weird flies (thank you climate change), many recent vintages have been minuscule. So pounce on any you can find. Some of them, like Maison Pierre Overnoy in the north and Domaine des Miroirs in the southern part, have become such rarities that they can be enjoyed only by collectors. You might find them on some wine lists, expensive, wealthy, but if you can afford a bottle and love the idea of ethereal wines, treat yourself. If you can't, don't despair. Though you'll need to work to seek them out, there are others at far kinder price points. If you love sparkling wines, explore the ones from this region, which can come close to the richness of Champagne. The white from the savagnin grape can be nutty and salty (see the last chapter) or like lemon-splashed oyster shells. The chardonnay, refreshing, light to the tongue but complex, an extraordinary expression of the grape. The poulsard (called ploussard in the hilly village of Pupillin) will be a little gossamer; the trousseau, a little denser and, depending on where it's grown, laced with rusty nail. This is a region that has it all for those lovers of wines that fly on gossamer wings.

The Jura region is a mere forty-five miles or so long and has a complex mashup of soil types. I've organized the wines from north and south. Don't bother looking for substantial taste difference—there is little—except the fruit in the south tends to be riper.

## Northern Producers

Domaine de la Loue, Domaine des Cavarodes, Domaine Bodines, Domaine Philippe Bornard, Domaine de Montbourgeau, Domaine Les Bottes Rouge, LuLu Vigneron, Michel Gahier, Domaine de l'Octavin, Domaine de la Borde, Les Granges Paquenesses, Domaine Pignier, Renaud Bruyère et Adeline Houillon, Domaine Désiré Petit, Domaine de la Pinte, Domaine de la Tournelle, Domaine Badoz, Domaine de la Renardière, Valentin Morel, Domaine Rolet, Domaine Ratapoil, Caves Jean Bourdy, Domaine Hughes Béguet, Domaine Didier Grappe, Domaine Gerard Villet, Domaine Les Dolomies, Sous la Roche Maldru (Thomas Popy)

## Southern Producers

Domaine des Ronces, Domaine des Marnes Blanches, Champ Divin, Domaine Julien Labet, Domaine de Buronfosse, Domaine Thill

# WINE FOR A RUNAWAY

"You know what? If you love him so much, go and live with him." My mother brandished the dripping spoon at me as if she really thought I waited all week to see my father. In those court-appointed breakfasts, she saw only my betrayal, not a powerless daughter.

I almost didn't hear her this time; I was too busy feeling even more sorry for myself than usual. When I'd come home from school that day—early because of a storm—my mother had been busy finishing up in the kitchen. Mom had always been sturdy in both form and function, but at forty-eight, she'd entered the brittle phase. Having lost so much weight since Dad left, she often scavenged my wardrobe for something to wear. She slipped into my Levi's for the first time in her life. It was a good look for her, even with that half-apron over them. She was stirring and chopping to get all the cooking done before she lit the candles. With just two of us, there was always way too much food, and neither of us hungry for any of it. It was going to be a long Shabbos.

When the mail finally slid through the slot in the door, I ran to get it. Almost everyone else in my class had gotten their acceptances, not that they were going anywhere great, either the religious Stern College for Women or the local live-at-home scenario of Queens College. Sure enough, there it was, the too slim envelope from SUNY Purchase, the only school I had applied to. I could feel my mother watching me, waiting for some response, and so I opened it. Never knowing how to hope for the best, I always prepared myself for the worst. I knew the inevitable. I was not going to be the next Margot Fonteyn or Martha Graham. When I thought of the audition, I felt humiliated. I'd worn an amateurish leotard that didn't even have a high-cut leg, like the other dancers'. For my choreography, I'd chosen an opulent, self-important piece by Rimsky-Korsakov instead of someone edgy, like John Cage. How could I, from the Hebrew Institute of Long Island and once-a-week training from Mrs. Lord, compete against the High School of Performing Arts kids? My mother did her best to comfort: "Don't worry, there's always Nassau." That was a community college where an old childhood friend of hers worked. Roz could just move some papers around, and I'd have somewhere to go. And all my mother was concerned about was my court visitation with my father. That was it, I was going to be trapped with her forever. Living at home. A loser. I was so screwed. I ignored her.

Jenny barked for a walk. I hooked her into her leash. "Zip up your coat!" my mom called out after me.

The dog didn't like being out in the weather any more than I did. It was icy snow, and the flakes, more like chips, were pitting my cheeks. Jenny was mercifully quick about finding a place to squat. We soon came back to the safety of the house, and the puppy shimmied herself off, spraying water all over the black-and-white tile foyer. Mom was waiting in ambush with a deceptively simple offhand question: "You're still going for breakfast Sunday morning?"

"Indeed," I said.

"He left you too, and don't you ever forget it," she yelled.

I knew why Dad left. I just didn't really understand why I had to stay.

Mom ignored the obvious, that I approached Sunday

morning with stomachaches and dread. There was little variation in scene or dialogue. The last Sunday, Dad had picked
me up on the corner in his little red Karmann Ghia, and per
usual, we went off to the Grand Diner, which was grand in no
other way than the name. He looked flamboyant in his side-
burns, thicker than ever, and his new fake-fur coat. We settled
into the red pleather booth.

"So, what's new?"

"Nothing."

"Did you hear from school?"

"No."

"I don't like this business that you only applied to one
college," he said.

"I didn't have the money to apply to more," I answered,
looking at him directly in the eye.

"I told you that was no excuse. I have the dough for this."

Our house was in foreclosure. He wasn't sending alimony.
And even though going to public school would have been a
blessed event for me, my yeshiva high school was threatening
to kick me out for unpaid bills.

"Do you think I'd let you down?" he asked.

When hadn't he?

The waitress in her blue apron came around to take the
order. "Now, young lady, what are you going to get?"

"I'll have the half melon," I said.

"Always melon," he said. "Live dangerously, take a little
cottage cheese."

Mom brought me back from reliving last Sunday's breakfast. "This Sunday, take these to him." She waved the brick
of bills she kept near the toaster. "I just bet she's there too."
She never used her name, Phyllis; it was either "she" or the
*zoyne*, whore.

37

"It's just him," I said. "Just him. He's enough."

She wasn't buying it. "You know what? You're no better than he is." Then came the same old lines. "Go and live with him, your great and good father!" she screamed. Consumed by grief and anger, I knew I was the only target she had, but that sure didn't make it any easier. She was hitting her stride when the phone rang.

Feeling like my veins would burst if I stayed one more minute, I ran to my room and stealthily grabbed the two tens tucked into my guitar case, my hat, gloves, and a toothbrush. I almost grabbed *The Bell Jar*, which I was in the middle of, but decided I'd just write in my notebook. I waited until Mom moved out of the kitchen. When I heard her take the steps down to the basement—like a sneak—I swiftly ran from my room for the front door and gently shut it behind me. I had often dreamed about running away, but I'd never had the nerve until I had nothing more to lose. I sprinted into the lashing wet snow with one thought: I had to go to the only person who understood. My brother.

The flakes were now the size of potato chips and melted as soon as they hit my glasses. It was a struggle to get to the corner of Adams Street and Grand Avenue, about a hundred feet away from our cookie-cutter split level. Then I imitated what I'd seen in *Easy Rider* and stuck out my thumb.

Within seconds, someone pulled over and my feeling of accomplishment was enormous, like spinning off forty-two flawless fouettés. The passenger-side window rolled down. At the wheel was a snow angel wearing a red beret and matching lipstick. She asked, "Hon, where you going?"

"Stony Brook," I shouted out, walking closer to the car.

"Get in," she said, and I was soon sitting in the passenger seat.

She lit up a cigarette, threw the match out of her window, then skidded back onto the road. "The roads are slippery, huh?" She acted like she picked people up every day, like my actions were completely normal and I wasn't some desperate runaway teen. "That's a long way to go on a night like this. There's not a better way to get there?" she asked.

It didn't take long for the sky to darken. It was the first time in my seventeen years that I'd dared to challenge the Sabbath's supremacy. In my house, all of my life, from the hour before sunset on Friday to when three stars came out the following night, there were no lights, no mail, no television, no stereo, no guitar. There were naps. There were books. Walks. And lately a constant stream of visitors coming to the house, as if paying shivah calls to my mother about the death of my parents' marriage. There was no escape.

The driving was treacherous. We hit the light at Atlantic. "I can only take you as far as Merrick."

Merrick Road was not more than one mere mile from my house. Who was I kidding? Hitchhiking to my brother in Stony Brook was as impossible as thumbing a ride to Paris.

She stopped at the red light. That was where I was to get off. "Good luck to you," she said.

I felt my failure but thanked my lift, darting out in front of cars as if daring them to hit me, and I landed safely on the narrow island in the road, trying to decide my next course of action. I looked across the street and saw a dim sign, next to the taxi office that said the Baldwin Council Against Drug Abuse.

I had been going there for about a year now. You could say I was recruited. On Saturdays during the summer after my father left, I'd take a sack of books after lunch and spend the day reading by the lake. After a few times, I actually met some kids. At first it was rumored that a couple of guys running around the park and talking to us were narcs. It turned out that Fred, a short, buttoned-up kind of guy with short hair and a tie, and the Zappa look-alike Robert, were legit graduate students from Adelphi University. Soon a bunch of us, drug users or not (like me), were hanging out at their smoky offices, playing guitars, getting pop-psychology therapy, and meeting people. I suppose if you get lonely enough, you'll do anything, even going to something called the Drug Council.

About to enter, I had the idea that surely someone would give me a place to stay for the night until I could make a plan. I pushed in the door. Once inside, my wire-rims fogged up. I took them off as I climbed the short flight of rickety steps to the top and a trio of small rooms. There was one office for seeing individuals and two other "rap" rooms. Even without my glasses, it was easy to recognize Robert, with that too big mustache that I had gotten used to and actually thought was sexy and reminded me of the older boy who had moved off the block, Peter.

"Alice," Rob said, studying my face, "you're not usually here on a Friday night."

I blushed; he had noticed. I looked down to wipe my glasses.

He put his hand on my shoulder and said, "And yet you're here now." He leaned down and whispered in my ear, "You're not okay, are you."

Already he'd shown more kindness and desire to really know how I was than anyone in my family. I joked, "Can I get some heroin here, to put me out of my misery?" I hooked my glasses behind my ears, looked up at him, and managed to stammer out, "I was trying to get to Stony Brook."

He thought for a minute and said, "What would you do?

Take the train from Baldwin into Jamaica and then take the train out again?"

I had never thought of that. "Nope," I said, and flexed my thumb.

"That won't work." Then he took a quick glance at his watch and stuck his hands in his pockets. "I have to run a group. Come. You can participate if you want, or you can just sit. When everyone leaves, we'll get some dinner and talk."

Rob and I had talked a little bit about guitars, about the war, about California, where he was from, about the Incredible String Band, but spend time alone with him? I sat cross-legged a few spaces away in the circle and tried not to watch the clock. Finally, when the others got up to leave for the night, I acted as if nothing could be more natural than hanging out with Rob. He handed me my wet parka and said, "Let's roll."

I assumed dinner meant the same shitty diner around the corner where I went with Dad, but Rob guided me to his Saab. I wasn't nervous at all; he could have taken me anywhere. We pulled up to the most exotic building in my neighborhood, the vintage, Miami-esque nubby stucco building with curves in all the right places. The Sweden Towers. I had always wanted to see the inside of what my mother used to call a "temple of traif."

Restaurants like that, low-lit and white-tableclothed, where the diners were polite and civil, were only in movies. I was used to Ratner's, noisy as a fish market, but this spot was full of library-like hushed whispers. There was an elegance, and I felt like a schlub in my parka, but grateful for my knee-high lace-up Olaf Daughters boots. I did my best to find another persona, the cool, independent kid, a successful runaway, a precocious baby intellectual who haunted the clubs on Bleecker Street.

Rob placed his long guitar-picking fingers on the back of my chair. It took me a beat to understand that even if he did have hair to his shoulders, he was well mannered. He is holding the chair for me, I thought with wonder. When we were both seated, he leaned over and asked, "Would you like a glass of wine?" I knew only from kosher and sweet. As if what I was looking at was familiar, I surveyed the options listed on the front of the menu. A scene in *The Bell Jar* popped into my head: Sylvia Plath's protagonist, Esther Greenwood, was intent on losing her virginity. Hours before, she had been picked up on the steps of Harvard's Widener Library by a pale math professor named Irwin. Esther decided to seduce him after seeing his study, with its "stuffed brown leather chairs, surrounded by stacks of dusty, incomprehensible books with huge formulas inset artistically on the page like poems." For her that evening, there were slippery snails that I could not imagine anyone eating, and a heroic bottle of wine. She tipped her head back and "poured down a glass of Nuits-Saint-Georges. 'You do like wine,' Irwin observed. To which she replied, 'Only Nuits-Saint-Georges.'" It turned out Sylvia had a thing about the dragon slayer. So that's what I looked for but I could only find a Rhine riesling and something called a Chablis. I had enough French to not call it "Chab-liss."

"Two," he ordered, following my lead. Then the menus. Among the shrimps and lobsters, I selected the small green salad and baked potato. He didn't try to push more food on me. But who needed it when there were chilled pats of butter sprinkled with salt nuggets for those soft rolls, like non-Jewish challah?

Green-tinged, the "Chablis" arrived in bulbous glasses. When he raised his, I imitated. I met his eyes briefly, then looked down at the wine, sank my nose into the glass, and inhaled for clues. There was something like pepper-flecked ripe green plums, not what I was used to drinking on Sabbath Friday nights.

"You look like a professional when you do that," he said.

"Smelling?" I was pleased. I must have done something right. "Everyone always criticizes me for that, but I don't understand why. You're not making fun of me, are you?"

"The nose is a tool," he said. "To warn as well as to welcome. We should all use it like you do." He gave it a try. "Let's add a little swirl too," he said as he swished the wine around and then smelled it.

I tried it. "The smells are more profound, right? It's as if they are released from the prison of the glass."

He laughed. I felt brighter. Sharper. Almost pretty. I took another taste. The wine had some sort of dry white plum flavor and was wet, which might seem silly, but it was wetter than water. I had no idea if it was as good as the Nuits-Saint-Georges, but it was more interesting than the sacramental wine I was used to. My cheeks warmed up.

With the sips taking effect, Rob did something no one had ever done. He asked about me. "Do you want to let me know why you are so very miserable? You don't have to, but I do want to know."

Did he really ask that question? Could anyone really want to know that I felt like the brittle wishbone between my parents who didn't care how many pieces I broke into as long as they won? Whatever winning meant. I couldn't tell him that, I didn't think I could tell him anything, which is why I told him that I would "rather talk about the wine," and took a sip. But then the story, at least about my day, dripped and then poured. He listened in a way that made me believe he heard and then I dumped everything else as well; how I felt like marrow was being sucked from my bones. He counseled. He understood. With Robert and that glass of wine, I mattered. When I finally looked around, I saw that we were the last ones in the room. The horses would turn to mice and the carriage into the pumpkin. He was going to do what was right, even though it was so wrong to me. He would return me to my mother.

The drive to Adams Street took no more than five minutes. He hung a left into the cul-de-sac and turned off the engine, waiting for me to get my courage. "Look," he said. "Here's what you're going to do."

"I'm listening."

"Your mom's friend can get you into Nassau? So go. It's not an awful school. You'll spend as many weekends away with your brother as you can. You'll do so well in school and write such a brilliant essay, you'll be able to enter school somewhere, away, as a sophomore. It's just one year."

"It might as well be a lifetime," I said.

He was quiet for a bit, then said to me, "I really do like you so much."

I made a grimace of dismissal and reached for the door to leave. I was being rejected. There was no place for me anywhere.

"Stop," he said, and wrapped his long arms around me, one around my shoulders and one gripping my head, pulling me to his neck. He smelled like snow. "I want to kiss you," he whispered to me, and I was yearning, please, yes, please. "I can't. But I just want to let you know," he told me.

Another responsible act, yet one that grew an apple-size lump in my throat.

"Thank you," I said, then threw my arms around him again and took his hug back as a treasure.

He waited until I was in. Jenny barked and wagged her tail, happy that I didn't leave her behind, and I heard Rob's car drive away. The candles had long since burned down, and my mother was reading at the table. She turned around to see me. Mom gave me a small and relieved smile. She didn't yell but gently said, "Come and have dinner."

"I already ate," I replied. My mother asked no more questions, not who dropped me off, who fed me, or where I had been for what must have been a lifetime of seven hours. She was terrified by my act of defiance; I saw it was beyond her ability to understand.

"So," she said, "okay, good night," turned back to her newspaper, and popped a pumpkin seed into her mouth, then another.

I motioned for Jenny to follow. I picked up the rejection letter and tucked it out of sight. Then I got into bed, turning around the wine in my brain, the adultness of it all. It turned out that I provoked no thunderbolts of anger from deities when driving in cars after Shabbos. But I knew this would give my mother more fuel when she attacked me with "You're just like your father."

Jenny leaped onto the bed and put her head on the pillow next to me. She certainly didn't smell like snow. With my arms around her, I went over every moment of dinner, like a prism refracting the light. The way Rob listened to me, the moment of the wine. But no, it wasn't merely that Chablis. It was hope. It was the future.

## DRINK THIS

Domaine Nicolas Faure
Nuits-Saint-Georges Les Herbues
Grape: Pinot Noir
Where: Burgundy, France

There's an abundance of attar. It's deep and sharp and with some blood and rose petal, the taste makes me think of a lovers' quarrel that ended well. At a slight chill, the wine refused to ask for a sweater; instead, it took off its shirt and just stood there, sparkling in the sun, a crushed blossom on a bed of clay. It loves air and breathes deeply. There's no knight slaying the dragon on the label. All dragons would have to be slayed in the glass.

Fate? Who knows, but it's so odd that on my first night out as a gauche seventeen-year-old, the theme was Burgundy. Keeping in mind what I drank at home, we're talking from the ridiculous to the sublime. I might have lucked out on pronouncing "Chablis," but I had no idea what it was. For example, did I know that it was a section of an exalted region? No. Did I know what grape it was made from? No, I did not. In fact, the only grapes I knew by name back then were Thompson—those pale green globes that came in seedless and Concord, which ended up in jelly and Manischewitz. Would I have comprehended at the time that there was no such thing as Chablis from California? Not a chance.

In 1971, hardly anyone who drank California Chablis knew the truth—that it was code for generic white wine. The grapes inside the bottle were most likely appley chenin blanc, a talented grape whose natural habitat is the Loire Valley and yet was California's most widely planted white grape at the time. But any kind of white grape could have been inside the bottle, because unlike France, the States had no restrictive laws of this kind. All of this appropriation stopped in 2005, when the EU stomped its feet protectively and won the right to own Chablis's use for chardonnay wine that came exclusively from vines around the eponymous Burgundy village.

Burgundy is southeast of Paris and under a two-hour TGV ride. The most renowned part of it, the Côte d'Or, is split up into two lobes, Côte de Beaune (southern part, known for whites); and Côte de Nuits (northern part, known for reds). Mâcon, a more low-rent district of Burgundy (home to great chardonnay, gamay, and some pinot noir) and the Beaujolais (chardonnay and mostly gamay) are farther south. To the west, just under Champagne, is Chablis, with its crustacean fossil-filled soils.

What I drank on that stormy night when I tried to flee

home with Rob was grapey and sweetish. Real Chablis would have been made from chardonnay and would have been steely, lemony, rocky, and perhaps even smoky, with tastes of green apples and oyster shells and brine, bracing and refreshing and dry. And yet what I longed to drink was the wine that Sylvia Plath mentioned in *The Bell Jar.*

*The Bell Jar* was published in 1963, only a month before Plath's death. When I read it in the early seventies, I was so impressed by what I took as the writer's sophistication. At the time, Lancer's was my idea of fine wine. I was so ignorant, I couldn't have known that Esther's wine had come from an eponymous village between Beaune and Dijon, from the pinot noir grape or that she had misspelled Georges (which does have an S at the end). Years later, as an older, wiser wine writer, I discovered the truth: Plath loved only the image, not the wine. It was even more apparent when I read the collection of letters written to her cad husband, Ted Hughes: "I drank the last of the vinegary Chilean burgundy, and I love you."

Syl, I thought, Burgundy can't come from Chile, any more than Chablis can come from California. Burgundy wine comes from the villages in Burgundy. Period. You can grow chardonnay and pinot noir anywhere in the world, but they cannot be called Burgundy. That region has a hierarchy of wines based on vineyard location—from simple village wine to Grand Cru at the top—and Nuits-Saint-Georges (sometimes abbreviated as NSG) is often ignorantly snubbed by label-focused collectors because it has none of the status Grand Cru designated vineyards. Nuts. The naysayers claim the wines can be a little rustic and lack the elegance of other villages, and perhaps they're not as long-lived. Yet for the record, I've had some thirty-year-old NSG wines that were mighty tasty, often earthy and philosophical, with a hint of spring. They can be serious and determined, worthy of a knight who must slay the dragon.

While certain pieces of land are more talented than others, if you have a good plot and work hard, the result can be glorious. This is the case with Nicolas Faure and his piece of land in a vineyard called Les Herbues.

Becky Wasserman, a remarkable American expatriate, moved to Burgundy in 1970. By 1980 she had a fledgling importer business that proved essential to Burgundy and those who drank it. Through the years, she and her husband, Russell, have graciously given me not only the most excellent of endive gratins, cheese cauliflower, and fennel soups, but also the basics of a priceless Burgundy education. One of the many times I stayed in her rural white stone farmhouse above the petite vine-packed hamlet of Savigny-lès-Beaune, her son and I went off to visit their latest discovery, Nico Faure. His *cuverie* was in the western part of Burgundy called Hautes Côtes de Beaune, just a few minutes west of the more prestigious pieces of the Côtes. A dark, handsome young man in T-shirt and khaki shorts, with his hands rough from work, he farms just under two and a half acres by design; he wants to be able to do all the work himself. He began his work at the most esteemed winery in Burgundy, Domaine de la Romanée-Conti (DRC). After several years, he moved on to the original radical winery, Prieuré Roch, based in Nuits-Saint-Georges, on the major road that runs through the wine towns, D974. Its late owner, Henri Roch (related to the Domaine de la Romanée-Conti clan) was the first Burgundy producer to make natural wine, little or no sulfur added, from breathtakingly expensive plots of land. In fact, one of the most delicious NSGs I ever had (and still dream about) was his 2006 Nuits-Saint-Georges Les des Corvées 1er Cru. There was no dragon involved but much fierceness in a salty wine with a fifties ladies'-powder aroma, with spice and cinnamon toasting on fire. Not a shy wine, it changed constantly and was blooming with the blush of life. I suppose one doesn't look for delicacy from this portion of Burgundy, but more firmness.

Nico's wines, for me, split the difference between his two mentors and is the talented new face for the dragon-slayer vineyards. In the cave, he had maybe six barrels for all of his wine. There was his tasty white, aligoté; his gamay, Coteaux Bourguignons Mes Gamays; and one mere barrel of Nuits-Saint-Georges. Where the gamay was all about *Drink me now,* the NSG said, *Hold on to me.* The Les Herbues vineyard is neither grand nor premier, but Nicolas has managed to create a wow of a wine that sure ain't basic. He uses a new (but old-fashioned-looking) press for his grapes called a vertical. You've seen these in people's front yards—they kind of look like a crank ice cream maker. The grapes are not removed from their stems but put in whole and crushed. Besides stems bring a more complex aroma and flavor, knitting in green and herbal notes to a wine that might be purely floral or fruity. Some critics view its effect as less pure, but I adore the resulting complexity. He doesn't identify as religiously natural—though his sulfur additions are a little higher than natural (certainly way lower than conventional), he works hands-off.

If Rob and I met up today and he asked me to choose a wine, I'd be at a better restaurant with a real wine list. If Burgundy was what I wanted, I might look for some beauties from the Beaune side (like Savigny) and even farther south, in the Mâcon. But the topic of the day is Chablis and Nuits, so I'd look for anything from these producers.

## DRINK THESE CHABLIS
## AND NUITS-SAINT-GEORGES

### Chablis

While the greater Auxerre region has sauvignon blanc (Saint-Bris) and pinot noir (Irancy), if it says Chablis, it's chardonnay. There's another grape that is extraordinary called aligoté. Once maligned as too acidic, in the hands of the pros like De Moor, it can rival (for me) the best white Burgundies.

Alice and Olivier de Moor, Domaine Caroline Marion, Château de Béru, Gérard Duplessis, Le Vin de Deux, Domaine Pattes Loup (Thomas Pico)

### Nuits-Saint-Georges

This is just one of the forty-four villages that go by its name in Burgundy. Pinot noir in the bottle, of course!

Nicolas Faure, Chanterêves, Domaine Jacques-Frédéric Mugnier, Domaine Henri Gouges, Domaine Prieuré Roch, Domaine Henri Naudin-Ferrand, Domaine Ballorin, Domaine Faveley, Domaine Arnoux-Lachaux, Philippe Pacalet

# READER, HE DIDN'T DRINK

Not far from the Normandy shore, Stephen and I pulled over to a little café. There really wasn't much choice. "I'm sure it's fine," I said, looking it over. It was our first meal that wasn't a picnic on French soil. We locked up our bicycles and went inside, choosing a table for two near the windows. "Does anyone eat out around here?" Steph asked.

I looked at my watch. "It's only seven-thirty, kind of early. We're eating on American time." But we were thirsty and ravenous. I quickly decided on a warm goat cheese salad, something completely new to me in 1981. Steph was going to get some local fish, *rôti*.

*"Et pour boire?"* the waiter asked, pulling around his waist the tie of an ankle-grazing white half-apron. With his finger, he tapped the card sitting in a metal holder on the table. There wasn't a full wine list, only the choice of a pitcher of white, red, or rosé. Suspecting I was drinking alone, I ordered us two sparkling waters, and for me, *"Un petit pichet du vin blanc, s'il vous plaît."*

The lace curtains blew in the salty breeze. Stephen took my hands across our little table, and we talked of the long bike ride from the ferry. The water and a spoutless pitcher arrived, the equivalent of a glass and a half. I immediately poured myself some.

"How is it?" Stephen asked.

I smelled it and said, "It's probably a little muscadet. But right now, it's my first sip in France, so it is absolutely the best thing I've ever drunk." I raised the glass to toast; he raised his water, and I tried to forget that toasting on water was bad luck.

Three years before, I had fallen for wine at the same time I fell for Stephen.

I'd moved to Boston for graduate school in the therapeutic use of movement. But the real reason was that Boston/Cambridge area was the States' hotbed for dancing. Not ballet but the folksy dances out of the British Isles and New England. Others went to discos; I went to the Central Square Church contra dances and English country dances, joined a Morris team, and danced every spare moment. I wasn't looking for a date—I was looking for joy. I first met Stephen—with his furry blond beard, flashing blue eyes, and wire-rim glasses—in the contra line, and I felt electricity the moment he took my hand. He was open and handsome in ways I wasn't used to. I had always been drawn to mysterious men who lived under clouds. Stephen radiated sunlight. We were perfectly balanced when we danced. That first evening, he sought me out for the last waltz of the evening. I was living in a Jane Austen novel with Stephen signaling intentions while we danced. This was not merely hormonal desire but a connection on a cellular level. Being with him was easy. And, he was kind.

We fell into the assumption that if we danced well together, we would do everything well together. But there were issues. While I thought I was too normal, he saw me as unconventional, more than he felt comfortable with. When I found out he was a lawyer, my stomach clenched. (Oh no!

Like my father!) He was from a working-class Boston Irish family. Catholic. My mother would never accept him. When she finally agreed to meet him, she quickly offered her verdict: "Ham on white." And after my father saw him drink milk in the morning instead of tea or coffee, he nicknamed him "the milk drinker."

In the spring before our European adventure, I had been laid off from the Victorian-era psychiatric hospital where I used my degree working with heavily sedated psychotic patients. I was depressed and broke. Yet Stephen wanted me to bike through Ireland with him. "Don't worry about the money," he promised. But the situation was fraught. My mother had brought me up to fear being owned. Even being bought a cup of coffee was suspect. How much more was a plane ticket plus expenses? I was beginning to understand that I'd be as alone as my mother was if I didn't learn that an important aspect of love or friendship was learning how to take and say thank you. Embarrassed, sure, but I accepted.

We left Boston with our bikes in boxes, laden with gear. First stop was Dublin, where, in 1981, the buildings were still swaddled in coal soot. The rain was incessant, and my rain poncho was useless. No one seemed to understand what it meant to be a vegetarian. B and B owners couldn't grasp that I wasn't going to eat eggs cooked in bacon grease. A little sausage in that cabbage didn't work either. Sure, the crumbly brown bread with the grainy tangy cheddar was delicious. But one doesn't live on bread and cheese alone, so when I saw a meatless cauliflower and cheese, I was initially overjoyed, it smelled earthy and pure but one bite told me it had been cooked into oblivion.

On our second night in a dingy room with polyester sheets that tugged at the hairs on my arms, Stephen asked me a strange question: "Have you ever been one place you thought you wanted to be in but wished you were in another?"

He was reading my mind. I said, "Yes, I have. That's exactly the way I feel. Can we please, please go to France? We're so close." I was thrilled when he said, "Yes!" Startled by this flexibility, I asked, "Are you sure?"

It took two days to bike south to Rosslare, and I felt like I was cycling downhill the entire time. I'd been fanatically tasting wine in Boston and had arrived at the crossroads where I almost understood how much I didn't know. In France, I was sure I'd find cheap restaurants with quirky wine lists. I had this fantasy that I'd come back to Boston not just with better French but with an improved palate. Maybe, just maybe, Stephen would discover that a bottle of wine was not a loaded gun.

Our ferry was an overnight. We chose seats on the deck. We spread out our snacks—sharp cheddar, seedy bread, salty chips, cashews—swapping with other travelers, chatting, laughing.

An hour into the trip, there was a dull but strong impact, food went flying and I was knocked over. Shortly after, the boat heaved and so did I, as did just about everyone else. I was bent over the rail, thinking if I just fell into the English Channel, all would be right. But Stephen, comforting me, wouldn't give in to being sick. He stood tall beside me, looking green under his pink cheeks. He gripped me, making sure I didn't fall overboard.

Morning came and we weakly rolled our ten-speeds and

stuffed panniers off the ramp into a lemony-colored morning, Normandy's Cherbourg. There it was. Heaven. "A market!" I squealed, seeing the spectacle spread in front of us. I was healed. Stalls upon stalls of produce, greens, fruits, potatoes, clothes for sale, food trucks stacked with tire-size wheels of cheeses. We stopped for francs, a bike map, and a lodging guide. Nausea transformed into hunger. We bought everything we saw, including a kilo of blushed apricots, all for next to nothing. I was twenty-six and couldn't see how life could get any better. It was nothing short of miraculous. My life had possibilities.

When the waiter brought over a warm sliced baguette, Steph and I had been congratulating ourselves for being so spontaneous. I asked for butter and reached for the tin of mustard, the color of a buttercup, on the table. Its sulfuric shock shot up my nose when I sniffed. "Steph, taste this. Why don't we have mustard like this in the States? Why can't they make bread like this in the States? Do you see this crust?" I asked, then slid my glass toward him and asked, "Wouldn't you like a sip? Come on, taste this place." I knew he would, how could he not? Then he slid the glass right back at me without even bringing it to his lips.

I knew that his abstention was not about avoiding drunkenness. It was about the control he had on the rocking ferry; it was about being a good boy. And mostly, it was about his father. The person he could never talk to me about, but his younger sister had, and I'd found out too many details about his family's brutality. Steph had escaped most of the trauma by melting into invisibility provided by study, fleeing into the protection of academia and Ivy League and possibility while his family burned. His inability to look at the devil, to taste the devil, made me fear that wine or any alcohol would be forever a threat. Yet in my selfish youth, I thought only about my needs and wants, such as how I was in France for the first time, with a man I loved, and he wasn't going to drink. He wasn't going to share with me what he tasted and smelled. He wasn't going to offer his opinion, "This was raised in wood, it tastes splintery," or "This wine spent time in cement, so vibrant." He wasn't going to say it sucked or it was delicious. We weren't going to giggle about our associations, and we weren't going to have that loose conversation that comes with the warmth from the fading anxieties and ensuing relaxation and then fall into bed. His father had stolen that from us.

A short pedal got us back to our home for the night at a run-down stone farmhouse. We walked through the gates, through the old orchard, the black sky encrusted with twinkling stars, and paused to look up. Fingers entwined, we continued down the gravel path and saw our host leaning in the doorway. The farmer wore a flat tweed cap and smoked a cigarette. He motioned us to join and led us to his living room. I imagined the wispy-haired man as a widower because I sensed a woman somewhere in that echoey room, but all of her touches had gathered dust.

Monsieur produced a small bottle and three glasses. He told us he was pouring Calvados made from his apple orchard. He poured, passed us the glasses, then toasted us for helping them beat the Germans in World War II. I tried to tell him it wasn't us, that our fathers were the fighters. He didn't care; we were heroes by association.

He plucked a sugar cube from the stainless bowl in front of him, then, just as my grandfather had before taking a glug of tea, he lodged the cube between his teeth. His hand, as gnarled as the ancient fruit trees on his land, raised the sturdy glass to his lips. He sucked the spirit straight through the sugar until the cube disappeared. How did the man have any teeth left? I wondered. Our host nodded to us, encouraging us to do the same.

*"Sans le sucre pour moi."* I picked up the glass he had poured for me, and its alcoholic heat mainlined down to my toenails. I sneezed, a common reflex for me. Then I sipped in the essence of apple on fire. *"Super bon!"* The taste thrilled me. I looked at Steph, silently urging him to taste it. He raised the glass. He brought it to his mouth. He pretended to take a drink. Then, not wanting to offend our host, I swiped Stephen's glass. I pretended I was just greedy and wanted more. Making a joke, I said, *"J'adore."*

That night in bed, snuggling up to Stephen, I said, "That was the first drink I've ever had where I was looking at the man who pruned the trees, tended and harvested the fruit, and shepherded it into its bottles. Can you imagine that feeling the farmer has?" I stared at the ceiling and out the window where the apple trees grew. I couldn't stop thinking about the fruit's transformation.

In the morning I bought two half bottles of the precious Calvados, carefully wrapped them in a bunting of old newspapers, and said our goodbyes. Stephen stuffed the bottles into his bags, carrying them for me over the next days of our trip until we arrived in Paris and parked our bikes, including those bottles, safely at our hotel in the Fifth. The hotel was an old one, framed by giant chestnut trees, in the bustling Latin Quarter, set back off Rue Jacob. Even though the bed felt as if it had been stuffed with chipmunks and their acorns, life seemed miraculous.

That first night in Paris, we chose Le Temps Perdu, one of those picture-book restaurants near the Seine, with white tablecloths, low romantic lights, and walls covered with old black-and-white photographs. I continued on my mission to consume every warm goat cheese salad I encountered. There was a wine list at this restaurant. As it seemed excessive to get a full bottle for myself, I once again ordered an anonymous small pitcher of white wine. Steph surprised me. He took my glass and sniffed it. "Mint leaves and tarragon," he said.

Was this the way a mother feels when her baby finally speaks? He didn't taste it, but at least he smelled it. Perhaps I could live with that, I thought. Perhaps I could taste and he could smell. We could share observations—it was the beginning of some new and exciting language. My heart was full of the possibilities. "Yes, you're right, tarragon!" My nose went back into the glass and added the descriptors of "Cat piss and cut grass?"

Stephen smelled again. "Grapefruit and a yew tree that took a bath together."

"I'm not sure what a yew tree smells like, but I bow to your greater wisdom," I said.

We walked out holding hands and giggling onto a bridge over the Seine. We stood at the highest point and looked into the river as the flat-bottomed tourist boats cruised underneath. He put his arm around me, awed by the glow of Notre-Dame and its steeple, seemingly ready for the hunchback to ring the bell. "We're in Paris," he whispered, and we were so full of the hope that comes with first times. He took me into dance position and waltzed me up and down the bridge.

On our last day, we walked the city. There was the Jeu de Paume and a whole lot of the Louvre. We found our way back on Pont Neuf and paused. He turned me to face him. He looked as if he had something to tell me. "What is it?" I asked.

"Marry me," he said.

I could feel a trapped bird in my chest. Did he say that? Truly? I hadn't thought about marriage until then, I was merely in love. With his proposal, the problems we had rushed me: My mother would sit shiva. His mother would scheme to get our children baptized. Would he become an alcoholic like his father? Was being with me too dangerous, was I a red-haired trigger with a wine bottle? But he loved me enough to marry me. Incredible. Perhaps we could do it. Perhaps. How many thoughts can one squeeze into an instant? I put my hand on his face, then in his beard, and kissed him. When I pulled my face away, he added, "At least someday I want to. Don't you?"

I ran away from him, toward the Left Bank. I heard him yelling, "Al! Al!" I shouldn't have been angry. He wasn't the only ambivalent one.

He caught up with me, pulled me to him, and buried his head in my shoulder. We gripped each other, knowing that we had no idea how to manage the love that we had. Something held us back, religion and wine a tried-and-true historical duo. I suppose people fighting and crying in public in Paris is what the locals expect of tourists; no one noticed us. When we finally separated, he took my hand.

We crossed the street to a cheese store. The cheeses were exposed, not under a glass cage. Moist air kept the disks and pyramids in perfect shape, oozing and dripping. We pointed at a fat cylinder dusted in black ash. There was a *boulangerie* next door where we bought a baguette. And then Stephen guided me to a wine store with the gravity and hush worthy of a library.

Stephen took charge. He used his nominal French for the first time: *"Avez-vous Sancerre?"* He had told me that when he was at Harvard, he had worked as a waiter for one of the houses that prided themselves on their wine club. That was where he learned of this grassy-citrusy-tasting wine called Sancerre. Made in the Loire, on the limestone and flint slopes of its eponymous town, the region was a three-hour drive due south from Paris. We bought half a bottle and a corkscrew. With our treasures, we took over a bench. He opened the bottle and passed it to me. Like the bottle the night before, it was minty. Far better than anything I'd had since I landed. He took it from me and swigged back. Then he kissed me, and he tasted like cut grass with notes of Stephen. He took another swig, as if showing me how it would be in the future, he'd take a bit here and there. If he could truly enjoy sips and smells and share the bottles with me even symbolically, his would be a most beautiful compromise. Yet it wasn't enough, and we broke up three years later for no real reason. We were just different species.

Steph gathered up our things, and we moved our picnic down to a patch of grass on the banks of the Seine. You could do that back then.

## DRINK THIS

Marie Rocher
Emmenez-Moi
Grape: Sauvignon Blanc
Where: Touraine, Loire, France

Marie's grapes come from vines she worked in and pruned; the wines were made in an iconic winery that shuttered in 2014. Anyone who remembers the Clos Roche Blanche sauvignon will feel this is somewhat familiar: savory deliciousness with some lavender honey and a beautiful integrated ripe-orange acid. Its ricey texture feels just right. Give this to a sauvignon blanc lover or hater and blow their mind!

Walking into my cheap hotel near the Oberkampf Metro with Marie Rocher's sauvignon blanc tucked into my bag, I asked the front desk, "Do you have a corkscrew?" I stuck the appliance into my jeans and walked up the stairs, prepared to contemplate my friend's first vintage.

I plopped on the bed and looked at the joyous label. It captured Marie in her "Let's attack life to the fullest" mode.

She and I first met on a morning in 2008 at a little café near the Gare de Nord to discuss my book *The Battle for Wine and Love*. She had just read it and wanted her dad, Jean-Paul Rocher, to publish it in French. She talked excitedly for the entire hour, her shiny brown hair rising and falling with each head shake. We've been talking nonstop ever since, usually about love and—what else?—wine.

Over the decade since I've known her, I've watched Marie segue from urban planner to bread maker to publisher to (finally making good on her promise to herself, upon her father's death) winemaker. And her first vintage was a beaut.

Marie makes wine in the center of the Loire, the Touraine (about two hours southwest of Paris) from both gamay (a grape I'm fond of) and sauvignon (which I am not). I fully believe that there are no bad grapes, only bad choices for planting and winemaking. But who cares what I think? Sauvignon is a beloved variety that thrills beginners because it is relatively easy to blind taste with its unmistakable smell, full of grapefruit, cut grass, and cat pee. The best examples are grown in its natural home turf, France, especially in the Loire regions of Sancerre and Pouilly-Fumé, but it's grown almost everywhere else in the world. New Zealand almost stole the Loire's thunder in the late nineties and early 2000s with its loud version. It was so popular that the Loire wine authorities actually hired New Zealand consultants to help make their sauvignon blanc more like New Zealand's. That's like asking Peter Max to teach Marc Chagall about color.

I don't mean to bad-mouth the poor grape, but I suppose I got turned off it by the cartoon variations. Speaking of Sancerre specifically, for ages there was only one organic and natural winemaker (Sébastien Riffault). Now there's a little bit of life, and I reserve judgment. Maybe one day I'll actually purchase one from that territory; back in those early days of drinking, I was known to enjoy one or two as well.

Marie is just at the beginning of her wine story, making wine in a part of the Loire I think actually outshines Sancerre— even to say that is sacrilegious. The Touraine. That is south of Sancerre, east of the Muscadet, southeast of Anjou. Château and goat cheese country. The soils are limestone, and the land is hilly.

I looked at my watch; I didn't have much time before I needed to go. I opened the bottle and smelled, tasted, and smiled. Her dad would be proud; I know I was. This was a gentle, rounder version of sauvignon blanc, so of its place, with just a touch of the green florality of violet.

Perhaps it's a little surprising that someone like Marie, who was brought up on completely natural wines, would add a smidge of $SO_2$ at bottling, which the most natural of winemakers eschew. But she has a fear of mouse. In French, this is *goût de souris,* a cute name for an unfortunate issue that is a retronasal smell (you can taste it but not smell it), making the finish of a wine taste like basmati rice with halitosis or kombucha gone wrong. Some added sulfur is thought to prevent the issue. However, Marie's wine behaved like a no-$SO_2$ wine; it was free, lively, and soulful. I knew it would get better over the next day, but I'd have to find out for sure when I flew home.

The next morning, I felt a little guilty leaving the sauvignon behind, so upon checkout, I gave the mostly full bottle to the woman who handed me back my credit card. "This is really good, I'd love to finish it, but I've a plane to catch." Then I ran for the subway to Gard de Nord and the train to Charles de Gaulle, just as I had the first time I met Marie.

It might be hard to find Marie's wines, as she doesn't make that much. If you want to explore this subtler, more complex, side, look for those from these fine producers:

## DRINK THESE LOIRE SAUVIGNON BLANCS

While Sancerre, Menetou-Salon, and Pouilly-Fumé are the most famously named regions for the grape (little-known fact: Sancerre and Menetou make a red and an even rarer rosé from pinot noir), there are not that many that fit my standards, and I often find much more interest elsewhere in the Loire, where winemakers might take more chances and, well, just be a little wilder.

### Touraine

In the Touraine, many winemakers will make a sauvignon blanc, but it's one of the very many white possibilities to explore. Among them are chenin, menu pineau, and the edgy romorantin (only "allowed" in Cour-Cheverny). Of course there are reds: gamay, cabernet franc, pineau d'aunis (rare but delicious), pinot noir, and côt.

Claude Courtois (one of the pioneers whose wines are always gentle), Julien Courtois (Claude's son; wines are more concentrated), Clos du Tue-Boeuf (another pioneer, makes a variety of wines and a mentor to many in the area). Zoë Puzelat (following in her daddy's footsteps, both are also using clay pots for vinifications like the Georgians). And don't forget Domaine du Moulin, Hervé Villemade, a neighbor and great friend of the Puzelats over in Cheverny.

Noëlla Morantin, Olivier Lemasson (recently deceased), Pierre-Olivier Bonhomme, Julien Pineau, all work pretty close to one another, near Marie Rocher, and make an assortment of delicious reds and whites.

### Montlouis-sur-Loire

Montlouis is next to Vouvray. While the region is mostly known for chenin, don't overlook the violetty sauvignons from the Montlouis-based Frantz Saumon and La Grange Tiphaine.

### Sancerre

Sébastien Riffault was the first organic grower and rebel in the area. Others you must know are Domaine Vacheron, Domaine Gaudry, Gérard Boulay, and the iconic Edmond Vatan.

### Pouilly-Fumé

Alexandre Bain (gentler but highly packed with flavor).

**Extra Credit**

Margaret River, Australia
Seek out Sam Vinciullo down in remote Margaret River, Australia. His sauvignon is a crazy, fun face to the grape with very low alcohol and lots of grapefruit-skin texture and zip.

# NINA MADE ME DO IT

"I'm shooting Nina on Sunday. Want to come with?" Herb asked.

Finally a Jewish man, but he sure wasn't one to bring home to meet Mom. He was too intense, too obnoxious, too handsome. He was also militant about drinking only white wine; maybe it was vanity, to keep his teeth white. More significantly, the photographer had twenty-one years on me and two and a half wives behind him. Even though I never thought I'd date a man named Herb, with a mustache, what could I do? Say no to Nina Simone?

There were three short days to figure out what to wear and what to bring while listening to "Lilac Wine" on her *Wild Is the Wind* album. There was just something, that Nina something, about the way she sang "I made wine from the lilac tree / Put my heart in its recipe / It makes me see what I want to see / And be what I want to be."

When I wasn't obsessing about what to wear, I was in Wine and Cheese Cask in Somerville, staring at the options, because I couldn't go empty-handed into the Copley Plaza, where she was staying in a fancy suite. Only bubbles would do. I'd read somewhere that she once drank five bottles of champagne in an afternoon. That was a very serious commitment. Working with dementia patients at the time, I was also on a budget, so I went for the champagne alternative but with a pedigree: a chenin from the Loire producer, Huet, something that had recently come on my radar, and it was gorgeous. A prize wine fit for a diva.

I tucked the bottle of Domaine Huet into my large satchel and walked four minutes to where he lived on a little street behind Sears, near the train tracks.

I'd first met Herb at a wild party in my old place on Huron Avenue. My roommate had invited him, her beloved photography professor, and he held court in our crowded kitchen, glass of white wine in hand, regaling his admirers with tales of hanging out with Miles and Monk. Who wouldn't be impressed? A compact man with precise movements, he seemed to be a terrific flirt, surrounded by eager women with hands on their hips. When he looked over my way, our eyes met and I felt shivers down to my big toes. Shortly after, I moved into my first solo apartment, on a cute quiet corner only two blocks away from his place. It really was an accident of fate.

He stood waiting for me in his doorway with a satisfied smile and a tic he had that made him look like he was chewing gum. I smiled, and he kissed me on the cheek chastely. Maybe I'd read this whole outing to Boston and Nina wrong. Maybe this wasn't a date after all. I felt even rockier when I walked into his living room, stripped down to its essentials, making me suspect an ex had recently moved out. But he came close to me, put his hand on my arm, and said, "Come. I want to show you something." With his hand fused to my elbow, he led me to his darkroom, off the kitchen. We pushed away the curtain; there were panes of hanging plastic and bins ready for fluids and the bitter vinegary smells of developers. He flipped on the light. Hanging on the walls was a Who's Who of jazz icons from when I wasn't even in kindergarten. I walked over to one shot, unmistakably Lester Young, a grainy image, shot at night; sax case in his hand and that flat hat on his head, caught in conversation.

"That was outside of the Five Spot," Herb told me.

A weary Louis Armstrong gazed directly into the camera, a Star of David around his neck, a joint in his hand. Then there was Nina. A studio shot. She was teetering back in a chair, optimism blooming on her face. "Where was that?" I asked, feeling a warmth of compassion just staring at the portrait.

"An outtake from when I shot the cover of her first Colpix record. We've stayed friends ever since."

"She was how old there?"

"About twenty-nine, I imagine," he said.

Just three years younger than I was at that moment, when everything seemed possible for her. I wanted that joy and power. I wanted that photograph too.

"Let's get this going?" He put on his leather bomber jacket and handed me my bag, surprised by its weight. "What do you have in there?"

"A bottle for Nina."

He nodded approvingly, lifted his two totes filled with camera gear, and we left his house for his rusted white car. On the drive to the Copley downtown I could feel the pressure of his hand on my shoulder, even though his hands were on the vinyl wheel.

I was nervous walking through the halls, I had no idea what to expect or what I could say once we got there. At her door, Herb knocked. The hotel suite door opened, and there she stood. Magnificent. A full-length mink coat worn as a robe swung open to reveal an ample body poured into an envy-green one-piece bathing suit.

"Herb!" she said in a velvet voice. She was taller than either of us, grandiose and regal. I smelled chlorine; she was fresh from the hotel pool. Her hair was swaddled in a towel turban. A huge ceramic jug of tea sat in the crook of her arm. Nina was on a health kick? Perhaps, and I was relieved that the bottle I'd brought was hidden away.

She brought us into the living room overstuffed with pillows and flowers. She drank tea, and she and Herb caught up, which was just fine because I was tongue-tied, too young to have anything of consequence to say. It was enough to be mesmerized by her eye fluttering and queenly composure.

Deep in my shyness, I nodded and watched and feared that Herb was wondering why he had brought this mute woman along. I was hardly eye candy or brilliant. Trapped in a job that was snuffing out my spark, my dullness embarrassed me and I had this growing conviction that if I didn't get off my ass and start my life as a writer, one day I would just vanish without leaving a thread of evidence. I was not the woman he had hoped I'd be.

Who knows how long I would have had that frozen half smile on my face if Nina hadn't realized I was sitting there in silence. She shocked me out of myself with the kind of question I'd more likely get from Shabbos-candle toting Lubavitch in Union Square and not the great Miss Simone. "Are you Jewish?"

I looked quickly to Herb for a clue of where she was going. But he was staring at his watch. "Yes," I answered.

"Wonderful," she said, and leaned over the couch. In a low conspiratorial voice, she asked me, "Have you been to Israel?"

After graduating from college, I'd flown there with my green backpack and fiddle. My mother had hoped that I would find the traditional prize—the nice Jewish boy of *her* dreams. It hadn't gone like that. "Yes," I told her.

"Excellent." She looked relieved. "I need an assistant who speaks Hebrew immediately. Be that person."

Did Nina actually like me? Of course, it was absurd to consider taking on the job as her assistant, but I toyed with the notion; maybe it was what I needed to jump-start my life and for the fantasies to ignite.

"You will come with me to see my best friend, Teddy Kollek," she commanded, then paused and cocked her head. "You know him, of course."

Jewish geography aside, the mayor of Jerusalem was not in my Rolodex. I didn't want to confess that though I'd spent twelve years in a yeshiva speaking Hebrew for half the day, I was far more fluent in French. Was she teasing me? I wondered.

Interrupting her interrogation, Herb said, "Nina, it's late. You should be getting dressed."

"I'm not going anywhere," she said, repositioning herself on the couch and pouring more tea. "I'm discussing business with Alice."

"Freddie should be about to go on in twenty minutes," he said of Freddie Hubbard, the horn player who was opening for her. "We should be leaving now."

The phone rang. Nina picked it up, listened, didn't say anything, and hung up.

The phone rang again. "It's George," Nina said, as if he were a husband she was bored with instead of the famed jazz impresario George Wein, who had booked the gig.

Herb snatched it. There was a lot of "Right" and "We'll see." He hung up. "Nina," he said softly and put his arm around her. "Don't worry. I'll be there with you."

Nina threw his arm off and declared, "Fuck George, I will not go anywhere."

While I had zero experience with celebrity, I did have some with difficult patients. Sucking in a breath, I told her, "I'd love to go with you to Israel."

With a victorious sigh, she removed her terry turban, then sauntered into her bedroom.

Herb whispered hotly in my ear, "She'll be two hours late."

"We're delivering her," I said, more than a little proud of myself. Perhaps I could be her assistant.

When she emerged, she had changed out of the swimsuit into a flashy sleeveless black and gold lamé top and a narrow black skirt, which she topped off with her mink. To make even more of a statement, there was another full-length mink in her hands and, to my eye, not even a hint of makeup. We were off!

We herded her into the limo, then nudged her into Boston's venerable Symphony Hall. Herb went to the main hall, leaving me alone with her in the wings. She did not look happy, nor did she show any indication she was going to go out there and perform. She folded her arms and leaned on the wall, looking at the stagehands and not to sounds of the audience clapping as they waited for their star. "You can do this. They love you. They really do," I urged, coaxing her onto the stage.

She was reluctant but she patted me on my arm and walked out to her spot at the piano. I watched, almost in a trance, as she picked the first notes and then powered through what I saw as sweat-dripping stage fright and not because she was draped in two fur coats. She caressed the keys and played as if trying to catch a tone poem, meandering. It seemed to me as if she were playing for herself, alone. She hadn't yet looked at the audience.

"Get back," the stagehand hissed to me.

I snapped myself out of sight and pressed my face to the velvet curtains. I peered out to see Herb below in front of the first row, in continuous-shoot mode as Nina's disconnection took on speed. She rambled. She spoke so low it was hard to hear. She played, harangued and invited the audience in and then

snapped them off. Then, without a look toward those ador-
ing listeners waiting, holding their breath, she stomped off the
proscenium. The audience was confused. Did they clap as if
that were the end of it or did they demand their encore? She returned, the audience, not knowing how to respond, went quiet.
She sat, she played, she talked some sort of incomprehensible
monologue, then walked off again.

There was a boo, another boo, then it was drowned by
some insistent applause as if to say whoever booed was a
jerk. She came back. Through it all, I could see that she was
unable to sing without feeling every note deeply and bleed-
ing through the songs of racism and love. As she rambled on,
I imagined she was trying to send me a message about heartbreak. That Herb might have been the only Jewish man I'd
ever gone out with, but beware love, beware attractions that
made no seeming sense. I had no knowledge which particular
demons she was at war with, but her performance was heroic.
As if giving a nod, a treat to a dog, her voice gave the greedy
crowd what they wanted: "I Loves You, Porgy." The collective sigh from the 2,625 people in the audience was almost
deafening. Full of benevolence, she led a mini-sing-along to
"My Baby Just Cares for Me." Were those peace offerings? I
wondered. Was it all improv, out of her heart, or the push and
pull of the performance and a strange sense of theater? What
a moving mixture of artistry through the madness.

The afterparty. No one remembered or cared about the late-
ness, no one feared tomorrow's embarrassing reviews. I finally
unloaded my bottle into an ice bucket. Champagne popped;
vodka flowed. There were platters of food, but who could eat?
There was probably cocaine floating around; none came my
way but the room's battery was fully charged and blurred. I
honestly cannot remember how the man who had opened for

Nina, Freddie Hubbard, trapped me in the bathroom, zoomed in for my mouth, and I escaped. I found Herb and my bottle, finally the right temperature, gulped in its lemony light, and whispered what I had sidestepped in the bathroom. Herb's amusement about my naïveté was clear. "Oh, that's the jazz world," he told me. "Worse was Nina's arrogance, her anger, her bitterness. She gave a miserable performance."

He was angry with his old friend and I couldn't understand his reaction. Obviously, Nina had been a wreck. He couldn't see that? My suspicions of Nina's fragility were only confirmed years later in a *New Yorker* profile and I did the math. When I met her, when she poured out her fractured life through her continuous interior monologue of pain, she'd recently come out of a psychiatric in-patient situation. I shuddered over Herb's lack of compassion and yet slid my hand into his.

It was near four a.m. when Herb walked me home, around the corner, after parking his car in front of his house. He kissed me, and there vanished Nina's warning and my misgivings as he kissed me again. For a moment it was the best date ever.

Nina didn't forget me. I received a card from Dr. Nina Simone. The return address was the Versailles Apartments in Los Angeles. In a frantic handwriting full of angles, she told me that Alberta, her latest assistant, had abandoned her. Forget Israel, she wrote, instead would I take care of her business and do her accounting? She added, "My left foot is getting cold from people's promises."

I couldn't have lived with myself if I had made her left foot even colder, but I had agreed only to interpret for her in Israel and not to run her business. Two years later, I packed up my belongings and Herb's gelatin print of a joyful Nina and moved to New York.

## DRINK THIS

Jacques Selosse
Initial
Grape: Chardonnay
Where: Champagne, France

While the Substance is considered the most coveted of the coveted Selosses, it's always too heavy for me and defeats the purpose of drinking champagne, to bubble along with the bubbly. But in this wine, I still almost taste the violet flowers running through the waves. This has verticality and a chiseled edge, like a well-honed knife, but the joy. The joy.

In the hectic week after Christmas, I was browsing the champagne aisles at a local wine shop. This is the best time of the year to pick up wild bargains in the category, as shops compete for the New Year's Eve customer. When I overheard a dapper guy in a camel hair coat and a splashy sunburned orange scarf ask a salesperson for a recommendation, my ears perked. The helper in a green apron reached for the predictable orange label. "I need to spend more money than that," the man said.

"What about Grand Dame? The company's top cuvée?"

I couldn't help myself and interrupted, "I think I can help you do better."

"Do you work here?" the camel-hair-coated guy asked.

Someone else passed me and said hello.

"No, this is my neighborhood store," I told the shopper.

"She's a wine writer," the salesperson said, and then turned to help someone else.

The customer held the champagne in his hand, and I asked, "Is it for someone quite special?"

"Björk," he answered.

"Yes. She is special." I didn't flinch. This was New York, where celebrity is a way of life, and I wasn't allowed to gush, but my brain scanned for the answer to what kind of champagne would please the eclectic, activist Icelandic singer. "And your budget?"

"Two hundred."

"Could I show you something spectacular for, let's say, ninety?"

He was adamant that he had to pay at least $150. I was mystified. Surely he wanted a wine that tasted great and was made with heart. Buy a well-advertised brand, like the champagnes that have product placement at every post–Oscar party table, and you are paying for their advertising budget instead of quality.

I could tell he almost understood what I was saying, as a publicity guy, which he'd told me was his work, he was in the business of yarn. So I told him a story. "A few years back, an old and dear friend of mine was standing with me in Champagne vineyards. Specifically, one of the seventeen Grands Crus, Avize, where they only grow chardonnay. On one side of us were the vines of Larmandier-Bernier." I tapped this bottle on the shelf. It was about $65. "Full of weeds and life. On the other was a sad vineyard sunk into hardened soil. My friend saw the little gravestone sign that marked that the grapes were going to Clicquot. Ronni pointed at it, grimaced, and said, 'I'm never drinking *that* again.' It was so sad, because she had loved the champagne, and in the eighties, it was actually pretty good, before Moët Hennessy Louis Vuitton bought it. She even served it at her second wedding. Look, do you eat organic?"

He nodded. He ate organic.

"Well, Ronni is an organic queen, as I imagine Björk is. Standing in the vines was her turning point. She understood she didn't want to drink wine that came from chemical-burned soils."

"All right, then." He was almost convinced that I wasn't nuts. "But can you show me something that is expensive, sends the right message, and comes in a box?"

"A box, a bottle, and two hundred dollars. Okay."

Sometimes only a box will do, which is why so many people go to Tiffany's instead of the little old jeweler who can deliver the same quality on the Bowery. Like a Tiffany, Champagne has stopped being a wine and has instead become a brand.

He put his hand on one bottle. "This?" he asked.

"If you want something that tastes like sugared dirt. That bottle is probably the reason why lots of people don't actually love champagne."

"Okay. So, suggestions?"

Surveying the options, I said, "Here's our objective: to let Björk know that you are not one of the sheep. And that you care. And that champagne is not just a symbol of celebration but tastes amazing."

I walked over to the minimalist bottle shouting at me: Anselme Selosse. "Now, this," I said, petting the bottle, "is the real deal. It has cult status among the people who care, so it has snob appeal as well as tastes damned good."

I dare anyone used to conventional champagne to drink that wine and not have a revelation of wow. "When Anselme arrived at his father's domaine in 1980, he eliminated chemical farming. This resulted in better-tasting grapes. He was the first in his region to rely on grape maturity instead of the norm: picking underripe and then adding to adjust for sweetness, a practice called dosage. His success was almost immediate. He was the first indie cult champagne and a father to a generation of new producers. Anselme changed the face of his region and birthed the 'grower champagne' movement, which means those who grow the grapes make the wine, the very opposite of what the big names do."

Why didn't my own diva, Nina Simone, get the Selosse treatment from me? Yes, I was aware of those champagnes back in 1986, but even though the wines were cheaper at the time, they were still out of my pauper's price range. I settled on the chenin from the Loire, made in the same *méthode champenoise*, from one of its most revered producers. Right, it wasn't champagne, but it wasn't shabby either.

I made him promise he would let me know how she liked it and gave him my card. I never heard back. But I'd like to think that somewhere in some fabulous loft in Brooklyn where Björk lived, for at least one night, she understood what champagne was and could be.

## DRINK THESE CHAMPAGNES

If the French have anything to say about it, and they do, only champagne can come from Champagne. The same method is used elsewhere, but the wine is called something else. "Traditional method," "*méthode traditionnelle*," or something similar will indicate the champagne method. Then there are other regions famous for their "champagne-like" wines. Included in these are Cava, almost always from the Penedès, Spain, and Franciacorta, from that region in Lombardia, Italy. But don't expect the same tastes and flavor, even if they sometimes use the same grapes, because Champagne is a region unto itself.

It's famed for white chalk soils, where their most coveted vines are grown. That's why England in the face of climate change, which sits on much of the same calcareous bed of soils, is being touted as the next champagne. It's more than just soil. Champagne is the definition of grace under pressure, survival in the face of adversity. Heard of the expression "making lemonade from lemons"? That's the Champagne story. Somehow, out of a dismal climate (snow in July? why not?) and the poorest of soils, comes a wine that triumphs. Maybe that's why Nina Simone, who came from so much pain herself, loved it so much.

Champagne is roughly divided into North and South. The North has been seen as the royalty, the South as its house staff. The North, with its famous cities Reims and Epernay, is closer to Paris. Northern producers use the classic chardonnay, pinot noir, and pinot meunier in blends or as single varietals. The South, closer to Burgundy (the Aube's Côte des Bar), which centers south of the quaint medieval city of Troyes, has its emphasis on pinot noir, and the champagnes can be more floral aromatically. So, why its second-class reputation? Because of politics. Near the beginning of the last century, when the region was being defined, the South was kicked out. A revolt ensued. People died. The region was reinstated, yet the tension continued. But now the hard feelings have been almost vanquished, and the South is vindicated and has proved excellent with imagination, independence, and having pushed the organic farming needle. Whether North or South, give these a try. They will be revelations.

**The South**

Aube and Côte des Bar

Bertrand Gautherot/Vouette et Sorbée, Emmanuel Lassaigne, Cédric Bouchard/Roses de Jeanne, Marie-Courtin, Valerie Falmet, Charles Dufour, Ruppert-Leroy, Olivier Horiot, Mouzon-Leroux, Champagne Fleury, Roland Piollot

## The North

Montagne de Reims, Côte des Blancs, and Vallée de la Marne

Augustin, Jérôme Prévost, Huré Freres, Lelarge-Pugeot, Champagne Bérêche, Emmanuel Brochet, Eric Rodez, Benoît Lahaye, David Léclapart, Champagne Françoise Bedel, Franck Pascal, Champagne Tarlant, Georges Laval, Laherte Frères, Aurélien Suenen, Aurélien Lurquin, Pascal Agrapart, Larmandier-Bernier, Pascal Doquet, Michel Fallon, Champagne Ulysse Collin, Roland Piollot, Champagne Marguet, Francis Boulard & Fille, Champagne André Beaufort, Bourgeois-Diaz, Stéphane Regnault, Mouzon-Leroux, Thomas Perseval

# FAKING IT

I was single, in my mid-thirties, and yes, I was broke. It was 1990, and to supplement my attempts at freelance writing, I had a very part-time job at Gracie Square Hospital taking patients to the roof so they could get some recreation and smokes. The ten thousand dollars a year I made from all of it wasn't covering my meager expenses. My rent was only $425. I learned how to make a meal from carrots. The bartender at Jerry's on Prince had become a friend and charged me for my small salad but not for my never-empty wineglass. And yet it was tough. I was staring at my cracked walls one February day, wondering if I should learn how to pray, when the phone rang.

"Am I speaking to Alice Feiring?"

"Yes," I said, then regretted it. It could have been a collection call.

"Great," the woman said. Hearing the kind of inflected English that spoke of private schools and summers on the Vineyard, I felt more confident that she wasn't looking for money. I wasn't prepared for her saying, "I'm the features editor at *Connoisseur* magazine. A colleague passed on your card, it says in quotes, 'One hell of a writer.'"

That card had been homespun and hand-cut. I'd written those self-promoting words myself and pegged them to the card's top. A made-up quote, desperate for someone to notice.

"I hope that's true," she said drily. "We have a feature here that we are hoping you will do for us. It's a wine story."

I had written a number of small articles, but no one had ever asked me to write a big wine piece before. I started to get this squiggly feeling I recognized as hope.

My brain raced with the potential. *Connoisseur* liked it fancy. I had visions of them shipping me to Tuscany or Bordeaux. Maybe Burgundy! The holy grail. "I have a million ideas," I blurted. I was about to launch into them when she interjected, "We need a piece on Long Island."

This was like expecting Domaine de la Romanée-Conti and getting Gallo's Hearty Burgundy. But then the editor added, "It's fifteen hundred words at a dollar a word plus expenses." If I had to write about merlot or sauvignon blanc on the city's most famous appendage, I would deliver. I agreed and hung up, screamed, clapped, and *boing*ed like a manic kangaroo. My jumping made such a racket that the heroin addict downstairs pounded on his ceiling with a broom. After two years of working in local newspapers and magazines for a couple of hundred dollars a pop, I would show my critical mother (real or the one that lived inside me) that I could make something of myself.

Fifteen hundred dollars might as well have been a million for all of the fantasies the sum seeded. I could take a friend out to dinner for a change, instead of being a charity case. I could pay three months of rent on my tenement and keep it safe. That was most important. To others, my apartment on the cusp of Little Italy and the East Village was a sign of poverty, but to me it was the life raft for the New York sea. It wasn't perfection. My ceilings leaked every time it rained. The floors were so slanted I could get seasick. And often, when I took a bath, so did the roaches. That editor's call was the fairy dust to keep me going. I bought new notebooks, made appointments. I was so elated, I could have floated out to the North Fork of Long Island, but I rented a car. I wanted the pricier Mustang. I settled for a Hyundai.

On a chilly Sunday morning in late winter, the roads were empty. The first hour of the drive from Manhattan with nothing much on the radio, I started to remember my kidhood. I was raised on Long Island's South Shore in a dull split-level on a dead-end street (which I took as symbolic). I hadn't belonged and didn't want to belong, as evidenced by not having those Long Island dropped R's and slouchy pronunciation. I don't know how I avoided them, except that I mostly spent my daily life daydreaming or reading. I was lonely growing up. The nearest friend was an hour away. Thank goodness for my brother, Andrew. But the scenery was dull, flat, treeless. There was no culture. No art. Brooklyn was where I was born. New York, which I longed for, was where artists and thinkers were created, not the South Shore of Nassau County, famous for houses made of ticky-tacky that all looked the same. (When my mother told me I could grow up to be a teacher so I could be home with the "kids," I felt so claustrophobic I couldn't breathe.)

Once I escaped, I rarely returned except for family funerals at New Montefiore and Mount Ararat. When Long Island wine initially emerged, I was not only curious but hopeful that, in the vine, Long Island (and I) would find redemption.

An hour after I left the expressway, the landscape gave into farms, big stretches of land, and gray and white clapboard homes. Pretty. My inn was a Victorian with creaky floors and a creaky bed but only fifty dollars a night. I dropped my bag in my room and went to see a couple I had arranged to interview: hippies hired to take care of other people's property and public relations. I softened. I liked them.

Larry Perrine was a Californian who had settled on Long

Island and worked at a new winery called Gristina (years later, he'd become the force behind the South Fork's forward-thinking Channing Daughters, that grew Italian varieties). That dinner was the first time of many that I'd hear about Long Island's great potential. Like Bordeaux's. Back in 1990, everyone wanted to be Bordeaux, one of the world's most famous and expensive regions. I tasted the cabernet franc. Not bad. Though it had a pronounced bell pepper taste, indicating that the grapes had not achieved full ripeness. Yet, I appreciated that the wine sang within its range. Everyone starts somewhere.

Returning to the inn, I laid my head on the pillow. That was when the insomnia kicked in. I had reason to worry. I had been curious about wine for a decade but trying to write about it for only two years. It was true that since coming back to New York City, I had drunk in every trade tasting I could sneak into and talked the talk; I had the gasoline of enthusiasm in my tank, but made no claims to be an expert. Actually, I had no desire to be expert. I just wanted to tell informed stories. While I could blind guess a pinot noir from a cabernet and a sauvignon blanc from chardonnay—who couldn't—I was self-taught and had so much more to learn. Then the words of my father came back to me: "Act like you belong. No one will tell you to go home." That was his take on "fake it till you make it," spoken like a true con man. But I was never very good at anything other than painting my emotions and fears all over my face.

Sleepless, I gave up, snapped on the light, and took out my pad, making sure I got the Long Island history right. Larry had told me that when the Wisconsin glacier receded, it created Long Island, with rocky, sandy soils. The southern tip of the island looked like a lobster claw, with the Little Peconic Bay in the middle, the Long Island Sound to the north, and the Atlantic to the south. In ten thousand years after the geological incident, there would be the first successful grape plantings. In 1973 after extensive research a young, enthusiastic couple determined that the area had the same maritime climate as Bordeaux. With temperate winters, the vines could survive. Frosts were delayed. That meant they could grow the so-called noble grapes of *vinifera*, especially the Bordeaux varieties, with some Burgundy varieties mixed in. Big-time grapes. The pioneering couple planted the first vines. The wise took notice. One of them, Kip Bedell, quickly followed their lead.

Puffy-eyed, I began my first day of reporting. The frozen morning grass crunched underfoot. I walked to Kip Bedell's modest potato barn winery, where a small group waited for me in a barrel room. Bedell (who, years later, would sell his place for $5 million) dipped a long glass pipette into the bung of a barrel to siphon off some of the merlot. He told me he had made some awful home wine and determined to do better. He wanted to buy a small plot of land to plant, but somehow that turned into fifty acres. He laughed, then squirted the purple merlot from the pipette into our glasses. I tried to look nonchalant but focused. I sipped, rolled the wine back in my mouth, looked for the wine's structure. Was it sloppy or did it have edges? I looked for the tannin that comes from time in barrel, the quality of the wood, but preferably from the grape skin itself. Fruit: Ripe or not? Red or black? Bright or leathery? The acid, that zing, so important. When tasting, we analyze those components, but the sum of the parts is more important.

Of course, I spat; otherwise, I'd have been slurring within the first half hour. But I wasn't used to shooting the wine into a plastic bucket on the floor. I felt as if all the others could see my imprecision and would mark me as an impostor. So much for my father's advice.

My fingers turned white and useless from the cold as I tried to take notes to describe what I was tasting. For sure, I was self-conscious, knowing they looked to me for approval. That was the worst, people waiting for my opinion, for some hint of what I would write about. Praise or condemnation. As if I could make them or break them, as if I were a fancy wine critic like Robert Parker. I wasn't. So, what could I tell them? Some of the wines were credible? Drinkable? "Nubile," I remember saying of a young wine, just a few months old. No one understood me. I tried, "You know, new, as yet unformed. Fresh."

That went over so well that I kept quiet as we walked the vines. I didn't let on that the closest I'd been to a grapevine was a cutting board made from one. I just watched, made myself sphinxlike, and tried to find some confidence, because at least I could find my way around a glass.

There were some palatable Long Island wines out there, but too many had undertones of their previous crops, potatoes with a whiff of corn and cabbage. I tasted weeds hiding underneath vanilla from the oak barrels like adolescents trying to cover up an acne outbreak. Others yearned to be simple, and yet they struck me as toddlers in tiaras, tricked up for a beauty pageant by hovering parents when all they wanted was to roll around in overalls.

On my last night, after three days of frigid cellars and vineyards, I was invited to dinner with Long Island wine's premier couple, who, a year after I had my first glass of "real" wine, had planted the island's first vines. Thirty-year-old boarding-school and Ivy League graduates, they began with a mere sixty-six plantable acres. The land came furnished with a 1660 farmhouse.

The wife was slight, like me, a bit taller, thinner, hair smoother. The husband had a doughy face and a close-cropped beard and was tall enough for me to have to look up to him. I took off my muddy shoes so I wouldn't dirty up their waxed wide-planked floors. They had art. They had Oriental rugs. They had a large dog with short curly fur. These people really did belong in *Connoisseur.*

In the seventies, the couple wrote a book on offal, way before the current microtrend of nose-to-tail eating, so I knew they were gourmands. I had made sure to tell them I didn't eat animals. "Salmon I hope is okay?" she had asked, and not wanting to be a bother, I'd said yes. As she put the finishing touches on the fat pink fillet, her husband escorted me upstairs to show off his real passion, rare books. When he closed the door behind him, I made a quick excuse for my exit and hurried down to play with their well-coiffed standard poodle and gab with my hostess.

Dinner was for three. We drank their fumé blanc, a made-up name out of California's Robert Mondavi winery for sauvignon blanc. They poured me some of their pinot noir, which I complimented, but when he talked about how one could mistake it for a Côte de Beaune Burgundy, it took all of my self-control to not blurt out, "Are you nuts?" Yet, as his wife talked, I could see her formidable knowledge. She was the one working the vines and had a sense of their souls. There was an appealing sincerity about her. He kept on voicing platitudes like "You can always style a wine to be sensational, but can it live to have a voice?"

Our chemistry was off. I tried to conduct my interview, and what I got was a public relations spiel. Just when I thought it couldn't get any worse, the lord of the manor turned to me. His eyes brightened as if he'd just had a stunning realization. "You know what, you look just like Woody Allen." Barbra Streisand might have been flattering. Nerdy, horn-rimmed Woody was purely nasty and suspect. His wife politely cleared the dishes, not knowing know what else to do.

• • •

I headed back home the next day, rewinding the Mamet-like dinner scene. What the hell did I do wrong? I had been in worse situations, and I'd be in far worse in the future. The feelings were the same: Shame on me, not shame on him, kept on repeating in my head until I dropped off the rental car on Thompson Street in the West Village. I walked the ten minutes to my building and lugged my overnight up the flights of steps to my apartment, appreciating my 670 square feet in all of its collapsed glory. The crappy cracked sink. The kitchen tub. My futon. My home. I opened a bottle of wine from the Languedoc that went by the name of Prat de Cest. It was simple. It was country. It was a local wine that just wanted to satisfy simple needs. Perfect. I took out my notebooks, turned on my Mac, and stared at the blank page, willing myself to write a story that didn't taste of soured grapes. My job was not to be critical but to get people excited about a new region, so the positive? The energy. The enthusiasm. I shaped the story as Long Island, a promising work in progress.

Once finished, I remembered advice from writer colleagues that personal contact with editors could only be a good practice. I slid my manuscript into a clasp envelope. I reached for my prized Salvation Army thirty-dollar 1960s black Persian lamb with a silver mink collar, absolutely the classiest fur coat a vegetarian could wear.

I got to the Hearst Building and headed up in the elevator. Once inside the office I pulled off my gloves to give my hand to the editor, Ms. Auchincloss, who gave me a smile and then a sideways once-over. Adam couldn't have felt worse and more self-aware after eating the apple. I had left my apartment thinking I looked the height of Lower East Side cool—you know, Tama Janowitz *Slaves of New York* kind of thing—but I saw her truth: I was using the wrong fork to eat the fish. I wasn't Woody Allen, but I sure was one of his characters. Blaming that vintage coat, I saw the future and understood I would be forever taking my patients to the roof to get their nicotine on. I didn't belong.

Four years later, off from Gracie, I attended fancy wine lunches where you never knew whom you would sit next to. This time, it was the past editor in chief of the then-defunct *Connoisseur.* He had moved on to a prime position at the Metropolitan Museum of Art and still did a little writing about the rich, which was why we were both at this la-di-da tasting featuring a prominent Tuscan producer. We discussed the wine, he nodded in agreement, we were both unimpressed.

"I did a story for you," I told him. He asked me which one, and I said, "Long Island wine."

"Ah," he said, "I remember that story. I liked it. You know, we were told by the winemaker you featured, 'That girl knew nothing about wine.' Some people, huh?"

My face burned, and so did my blood as I said to myself, It wasn't my coat after all.

By 2000 the winemaking couple had sold the winery and had divorced. Long Island carried on. I came to understand that not everyone could blind taste one variety of grape from another. When asked to write about the world's most overrated wines and regions for *GQ,* I thought about it hard and then decided that I had to include Long Island. What did I say? "The strawberries, potatoes, and corn grown out on Long Island are world-class. But grapes? Not so much (though you've got to give local winemakers credit for their perseverance)."

## DRINK THIS

La Garagista
In a Dark Country Sky
Grape: Marquette
Where: Vermont, USA

Marquette, a super-new hybrid grape, was born in 2006 with eight different *Vitis* in its history. One of its parents is said to be the exalted grape, pinot noir. The wine is seductive, sharply focused with a beautiful high-pitched verve of frosted roses and spiced cherry, or think of it as a more natural cherry cola than in my youth, but without the sugar. A savory, yummy, "oops it's gone" kind of refreshment that makes you want to head to your favorite mountaintop and breathe in deep? Yes!

If you had told me ten years ago that the state mostly known for Bernie's mittens, Ben & Jerry's, and tapping maple syrup was going to be America's most celebrated wine region, I would have said, "Sure. By the way, may I interest you in a bridge I have for sale?" But Vermont has done what Long Island did not, given birth to true local wines and shown that local and great are not mutually exclusive.

Want analogies? Think *cucina povera*—foods of peasant culture—pizza, pasta and simple tomato sauce, simple foods made by humble people, identified with their country or locale, and so delicious we can't stop licking our plates and fingers. The best of local food and wine hits the sweet spot for comfort. So, when Long Island had set out to imitate Bordeaux (not unusual for a region to model itself on some other region's success) instead of seeking its real identity, the decision felt off. When a region does that, it puts on airs, and the result can ring so false. Imitation comes off like a bow tie on a warrior, or the way I always felt in teetering high heels, kind of ludicrous.

But Vermont. Now, there is a case study in how it was done right.

Remarkable flavors come from regions on the cusp of the ability to grow grapes—hello, Champagne? Likewise, Vermont has fantastic soils and a marginally cool climate. The state also has a very rare benefit: arable land is affordable without needing to sell one's firstborn to the highest bidder. While on Long Island or around most of the United States, new winemakers must be trust-funders to buy land, but in Vermont, it is possible to get a few acres even without a wealthy spouse or family money. Hallelujah.

Yet Vermont's nascent wine industry had a massive image problem because they planted hybrid grapes. Sure, Vermont's natural resources spoke of talent, but they needed vines suited to their climate-challenged state—cold, wet, muddy, with a short growing season and black flies. They needed a vine that could survive hardships. To select a variety for status or fashion would be a fool's choice. Sensible Vermonters nixed the fragile, fancy *vinifera* like merlot and chose cold-hardy hybrids like marquette. These hybrids were invented by botanists who cross "noble" grapes (called *Vitis vinifera*) with native American ones, either *labrusca* or other kinds of *Vitis*. Culturally, hybrids have been accepted for jams or home gardens but rejected for fine wines, criticized as tasting too fruity and often too grapey, with a touch of wildness called "foxiness." At first, the natives apologized for their grape inferiority. In those early days of their wine industry, tourists enjoyed sipping in Vermont tasting rooms but never thought of drinking these wines at home.

That all changed with Deirdre Heekin. With her wavy blond hair and strength of spirit, Heekin will one day be seen as the godmother of Vermont wine.

Her path to winemaking was long and winding. She and her husband Caleb ran a beloved restaurant in Woodstock, Vermont, Pane e Salute, where they used their own farmed ingredients as much as they could. Deirdre grew apples; she fermented cider. She noticed wild grapes everywhere and thought, why not put in some vines. As farming took over her life, she inched toward releasing her wines into the market, acquiring more vineyards along the way. In 2017, after two decades, the couple closed their restaurant and devoted themselves to their winery, La Garagista.

Deirdre was convinced that she could express something unique from once-maligned fruit by using close observation and sensitive farming. She was right. Before her, the local farmers would say that organic grape farming was impossible. Before her, no one would think of ordering a Vermont wine, or a hybrid wine, let's say in Copenhagen, New York, and Paris wine bars, as they do now.

The La Garagista wines are considered "natural." Natural wines start with organic or equivalent farming and have none of the more than seventy-two legal additives, except a minute amount of sulfur. However, Deirdre goes a step further. Her wines are considered zero/zero natural: no additives in the vineyard or the wine, not even the sulfite addition. She vinifies in neutral, unromantic vessels like food-grade plastic bins, old oak, and clay to maximize the grape-alone element.

Since 2011, when I started tracking her wines, those grapes—with sassy names like Louise Swenson, brianna, frontenac, and la crescent—have had more to say about where they came from. Delicious, snappy, crunchy, fun. Because of her work, it's near impossible to make wine in Vermont any other way than naturally and be taken seriously. Deirdre has birthed a thriving community of people following in her footsteps, putting their local wines (with such freshness they taste like gulps of mountain-fresh air) on the map. Their simple wines have become great, though greatness was never the objective.

### Drink These Northeast Local Wines

What intrigues me about the wines from the United States Northeast is that they are happy to find their own way. While they might take inspiration from other regions, they are seeking their own special identity. Oh, and don't forget the cider!

Vermont: Slide Show, Iapetus, Elliston Estate Vineyard, La Montañuela, Stella 14, La Garagista, Kalché, Chertok

Finger Lakes: Chëpìka, Bloomer Creek Vineyard, Eminence Road Farm, Hermann J. Wiemer Vineyard, Usonia

Hudson Valley: Wild Arc Farm

Long Island: Floral Terranes, Channing Daughters (more will come, but right now most are catering to the tourist trade)

Quebec, Canada: Pinard & Filles, Vignoble les Pervenches, Domaine du Nival, Hinterland Wine Company, Pearl Morrisette

# Water of Life

The snow piled high on our hats. I cried out as I fell into a drift in near-whiteout conditions.

"Why the hell did we come to Poland?" I asked.

"Because I made you," Melissa said weakly. I told her to hold tight. We were going to get out of Birkenau alive.

It really was Melissa who had persuaded me to come along with her to Poland on a Belvedere distillery–sponsored trip in 2004.

Poland. In the winter.

She and I initially bonded at a Barolo tasting in New York City, realizing that not only had we both been rereading *Daniel Deronda* for the third time, but we were aligned in the way we perceived taste. "Do you taste chicken soup?" she'd ask about the tempranillo. "Yes! With dill," I'd answer. And then, besides seeing wine through the same taste buds, we were also Jews in the not-so-Jewish world of food and wine writing.

Melissa was more than a decade younger than I was. We began to travel for assignments together, passing as red-haired sisters. While chasing our stories, we had other shared priorities: food markets, wine shops, wine bars, museums, and yes, a sale here and there. Our pace was synchronous except for one thing—she could go into churches to look at the art for hours, while I saw one Madonna and a few angels and was done. We usually traveled on our own dime or on a meager allotment for expenses. We stayed in spartan hotels, took the cheapest trains, and rented the mini-est cars, saving our money for food and wine. We cherished our memories of the intensely mango-colored egg yolk smothered in shaved white truffles in Piemonte, Italy, and the time we wondered if anyone would ever pick us up as we hitchhiked to the ferry to the Isle of Skye in Scotland. Independence was insurance that our opinions couldn't be bought, which was worth traveling like refugees. Yet every once in a while, a press trip came along that made us want to bend those convictions because it was attached to an assignment. Sometimes we massaged our rules because we had ulterior motives. Look, she didn't want to cover the new "orange"-flavored Belvedere vodkas any more than I did. But she did want to go to Auschwitz. "When else would we go?" she asked.

Like, never? For someone who habitually looked back on her life and history with a microscope, I was oddly not interested in seeing where my people came from. As far as concentration-camp tourism, I would rather listen to my cousin Sarah's stories. "But Auschwitz?" I asked. I'd heard it had been turned into a very commercial museum. "I don't think I have the stomach to see the spit and polish, the sanitization of horror."

"Oh, come on," she urged.

So I bargained. "I'd rather go to Majdanek."

That camp was personal to me. It was the one that Sarah and her family had escaped from. I had never found anything about this breakout in holocaust history, but Sarah told it in such detail, I never doubted its veracity. However, it was just too far away, and since we didn't want to extend our stay, I gave in. "Okay. But if we do Auschwitz we'll also have to do Birkenau." I had read there was no visitor center, there was no guided experience, just the empty camp.

We arrived at a cushy hotel in Warsaw with a latent Soviet edge. The first night, our host treated us to a fancy meal in a park, and as I took bites of smoked fish and herring, I found the taste sentimental. I pushed a note to Melissa: "As good or better than Russ & Daughters?" She scribbled, "Better." The food woke up memories. That night I had nightmares peppered with all of Sarah's stories.

The next day, teeth clicking with the cold, we found our seats on the slow, rattling train to Żyrardów. The heat on the train wasn't bad, and our hats came off as we shuttled by the flat, dull, and snowy landscape, where once shtetls roamed. It was as flat as a potato pancake, and scenes from my cousin's life kept filling up my head. "I can't stop thinking of Sarah," I said to Melissa.

She looked at me and motioned for me to tell and I continued.

"Shortly after she and her family were moved into Majdanek, there was a guard who agreed to help the inmates. He told them one night would come when he would open the gates for three minutes. Whoever could would run out as fast as they could. After three minutes, he would unleash seven dogs, who would race after them, but only seven people could be caught. Everyone else would have a chance to escape.

"The signal finally came. Sarah, her mother, father, brother, and a friend made it through the woods to a neighbor's house in Lublin, which was only under a two-hour walk away. There they were able to procure phony papers, bleach Sarah's dark hair, and separately board a train to Warsaw. Ten minutes into the journey, the train screeched to a stop. Five Gestapo got on the train, shining flashlights in the passengers' faces as they began checking identification. A peasant sitting across from my cousin whispered to her in Polish, 'Jew.' Sarah knew that the peasant could get a year's worth of money for handing her over to the officers, who were about to approach. The man on Sarah's left, whom she hadn't even noticed, addressed the peasant forcefully but quietly, 'Bitch, if you value your life, you will shut your mouth.'"

Melissa closed her eyes and asked, "And then?"

"The Germans handed Sarah's papers back, saying, *'Auf Wiedersehen, Fräulein.'* But from the back of the train, she could hear others being identified as Jews. Sarah heard the voice of the friend, along with several others, being taken out of the train. She heard the shots but did not look. In the commotion, the stranger who had protected my cousin disappeared."

Melissa shivered, hugged herself, looked out the window, then behind her.

As we walked to what had become the Belvedere distillery, we had the irrational fear of being pulled over and shot. Of course, it was nonsense, because as journalists in Poland in 2004, we were well received; no one asked us to show them our yellow stars. In a few minutes we were smiling politely and sitting in front of a friendly woman in a tight skirt, who explained the company history as we scribbled notes.

The Belvedere distillery was founded in 1910 by the Pines family, she said, pronouncing their name "penis." Like eighth-graders, we couldn't stop giggling. "They were a Jewish family," she added, and I thought, Of course. Before the war, Jews, often seen as nondrinkers, were involved in booze, and 75 percent of Poland's distilleries were owned by them. Jews even owned taverns.

She continued the history with the next phase. "The Daumans bought the place in 1924, and in 1932 they turned it into the most modern distillery in the country. In 1939 the factory provided vodka for the 'war effort.'"

"Dauman? That's not a very Polish name," I said, suspecting the family's truth. "Where were they from?"

"They were Jewish," she said.

That wasn't my question. Of course they were Jewish. At the time, I assumed what I would later find out was correct, that the entire family was murdered in Auschwitz. Ignoring any sense of politeness, I asked, "What would it take to put a plaque up, to commemorate the original owners, something like, 'In memoriam for the Dauman family who created this distillery, seized in 1939, and they were sent to their death. May their memory be a blessing.' How hard would that be to do?"

Obviously, impossible. The story of what happened to the Belvedere founders was the story I cared about, not the mythology, or that Belvedere had to be made with local grain or potatoes or Polish water to be a superpremium and pure vodka. I didn't want to hear anything about the word "purity." I wanted to hear about the Daumans.

We took the train back to freezing Warsaw and walked toward our hotel on the main square. Fixated on the Jewish origins of the distillery, I persisted in talking about it. "What is Belvedere worried about? That the family would come back and ask for reparations? That the anti-Semites of the world would not buy their vodka? Or were they just hoping to erase memory?"

Our lips were turning blue. I had an inefficient down coat. Melissa had a cloth one. "That's not going to get you through Auschwitz," I said, like a mother. Well, she did have her aunt Sandy's mink hat, and I had my bunny-lined Mad Bomber. We both had long underwear and not that much flesh on us.

This was no way to dress for Warsaw in early February. Since we had seen that the city had plenty of vintage shops, we had the idea to find extra layers for cheap.

The shop we found smelled of camphor and was packed with treasures. Bags of vintage shoes. Silver. Light fixtures, exquisite glassware. Racks of old furs. We both reached out to touch one salt-and-pepper Persian lamb but stopped as if its skin had turned into porcupine quills. The dead were everywhere. We fled. "What were we thinking?" I asked.

"I don't know. I don't know."

I had not taken time to be analytic. Were those shoes from the thirties and forties? Or was the fur safe, from the fifties and sixties? We should have examined it more closely. It didn't matter; everything there could have been purloined objects from those sent to their death.

"Let's just accept the cold," Melissa suggested, linking her arm in mine and pulling me toward the hotel. "And let's get a drink."

We took refuge in the bar. Only fifteen years after the fall of communism, as I looked at the waiter who brought over cubes of creamy feta and soggy green olives, I thought, at one time he could have been Stasi.

Melissa grabbed the wine list. I asked, "What do they have?"

She saw the truth. "There's nothing but Gallo and Turning Leaf. We're sunk."

We ordered vodka made from potatoes. Luksusowa.

I never connected my love of drinking to my roots. One doesn't think of wine and Poland. The Little Ice Age in the nineteenth century pretty much stopped Poland's winemaking. There are some vines even today not far from Warsaw. Sarah remembered that in her youth, there were vineyards where she summered in the Carpathian Mountains. But real wine was rare in the shtetls, where our relatives often made sacramental wine from raisins. There was plum brandy, slivovitz, but it was vodka that defined local life. Even in the ghettos.

In 1941 Sarah and her family were moved out of the Lublin Ghetto into Majdanek Tatarski, the temporary village bordering the Majdanek concentration camp, in the process of being built. In other words, the Jews were forced to build their own death camp. While the building was in process, in the morning, some were marched onto the grounds, while others, like Sarah and her family, were marched into Lublin for office or factory work. Their breakfast and probably everyone else's kicked off with a glass of vodka. "Vodka was better than bread, and anyway, often it was the only choice," Sarah explained. It was undoubtedly more warming in the winter mornings. And if you don't drink too much, the initial hit invigorates. On the dawn marches, Sarah remembered how the local Poles would jeer at them, but they also held up bottles for sale. Her family knew that vodka was a great bribe, and those with a bottle stash had a better chance for survival. The lucky, like Sarah's parents, who had managed to hide away some coins were able to buy a bottle, sometimes two—one for the Wehrmacht soldier guarding them. This gave "water of life" another meaning.

"Melissa," I said, taking a swig, "have you ever read of the nightclubs in the ghetto?" I hadn't until I worked on Sarah's memoir. There were clubs in both the Warsaw and Lublin ghettos, probably everywhere else as well. Drinking was a way of living and surviving and dealing. "Sarah was in love with a boy named Judah. When they were moved into Majdanek Tatarski, she told me that every night, the kids had drunken parties where they'd joke, 'Which chimney do you want to go up in?'"

After liberation, my grandmother and her sisters, safely in New York, found Sarah and her parents and sponsored them to immigrate to the United States. Sarah told of a care package that they received from their newly discovered relatives. "There were things there that we had never seen. Peanut butter and canned pineapple, what were those?" She laughed at the fancy nightgowns from a relative who had manufactured them. In the postwar shambles, such froufrou was absurd.

Sarah was so very different from my mother. Sarah embraced life while my mother feared it. My mother hated heat more than cold and was happy for most of her life to be alone. Sarah also never lost her intolerance for the cold or her need for people. Sarah's memories were everywhere. I couldn't turn them off. I told Melissa more. "After her husband, Sasha, died she was frank with me about how, while Sasha was the love of her life, she was not going to be alone and she did remarry a good man, but not a Sasha, as soon as she could. That new life experience entitled her to give love advice. From Sarah, I didn't mind. I remember her saying in her crackling Polish accent, 'Honey, let me tell you.' And then she would go on to explain that it was essential to have dinner with your husband or lover at least five times a week. She tried to teach me about flattering a man's ego, something I never was good at. She was the only one in my family who drank with a sense of vitality and community. Vodka was her wine."

"So when your mother says, 'How do you come to wine,' tell her it comes from Sarah's side of the family. It's in your blood," Melissa said, and knocked back her drink for emphasis.

On our last day in Poland, we hired a taxi in Kraków to take us to the camps an hour away. As we drove, the falling morning snow gathered on the trees and looked like wintry mimosa blossoms. We arrived at the gates, and the taxi driver instructed us that he'd be at the camp's café, so we should look for him there when we were ready to leave.

The *Arbeit Macht Frei* looked so much smaller than in the pictures and movies. Tiny but powerful, and it silenced us. We paid for our tickets and began our self-guided tour. A sign pointed to visitor toilets behind the crematorium. We went inside the shower room, which seemed as small as my living room, but I thought my mind must have been playing tricks on me, as I felt the ghosts of hundreds of bodies packed in, like tinned fish. Zyklon B smelled like marzipan or bitter almonds. "Can you smell anything?" I whispered. There we were, two of the best noses trying to sniff the past. Had the Dauman family died in that room? It was inconceivable that even though it had been sixty years ago, there wasn't a trace of the stain.

The narrow lanes between the brick buildings were slippery under the light snow. Some locals had shown up. The woman we were watching was a gorgeous model type with a leopard tote bag and Versace-esque ecru high-heeled leather boots (in the snow! spikes!). She laughed and romanced her companion as they tromped through the pretty snowfall. I whispered to Melissa, "This is an outing for the locals?" We were incredulous, as they seemed out for a romp at the camps. Another handsome couple played with their toddler. I could envision the local *Time Out* promoting spring picnics or singles events at Auschwitz. Why not? Buildings where German officers had been housed had been turned into museums. "Blame it on the Germans" was a popular theme. The one building dedicated to the "Jewish Martyrs" was bolted shut.

"Can we get out of here?" I asked Melissa. She'd had had enough too. We went to the fancy toilets, not the ones behind the crematorium, skipped the gift shop, and found our driver. As we settled into the backseat, the driver asked, "Why do you want to go to Birkenau? There's nothing there."

"That's why," I said. "We want that nothing."

However, it was everything. The iconic train tracks leading right into the camp looked sinister. There was no signage. There were no people. We climbed the stairs to the observatory in the watchtower over the train entrance. Up from that pigeon's perch, the camp looked huge, a barren, treeless vista with rows of malignant-looking barracks. My brain swam with other people's memories. We studied the map, and when we had a sense of the camp's layout, Melissa and I set out to explore.

The air was arctic. We zigzagged through the snow—there were no paths, and we had no boots. We arrived at the row of low buildings, wooden barracks, and chose one to enter. The door easily opened to a room of large wooden bunklike shelves for beds that could cram in sleeping bodies. The room reminded me of the chicken coop my grandfather worked in on the Lower East Side. Melissa and I, both nearsighted, crept close to the wooden slats that separated the bunks to examine the graffiti scratching of desperate prisoners. Though I could read some Yiddish, I couldn't understand any of the meaning, yet instinctively pressed my fingers to the wood to feel the carvings, trying to touch the writer's hands. Melissa and I didn't talk. We just looked. Examined. Breathed.

We left for where the crematoriums that once processed two thousand bodies at a time had stood. I read that word somewhere, "processed." In 1945 the Nazis tried to destroy much of the incriminating evidence of the killing, so all that was left of the incinerator was an enormous chimney peeping out of the snow. "The snow is really coming down," I said. My feet had turned into chunks of ice. My fingertips were senseless; my nostril hairs were icicles. We were finally ready to leave. Melissa fell in the snow, and we realized we were lost.

For twenty minutes, my feet felt frozen to the ground, yet I managed to move them as we searched for the gate, and my blood pressure rose. "Can you imagine the irony?" I asked. "Sarah survived the Lublin and Warsaw ghettos, escaped the Majdanek camp, survived typhoid and bayonets and attempted rape, the walls of a Warsaw home, countless peasants wanting to turn her in, the death of her two brothers, and people being killed in front of her, and we're going to die in Birkenau because we're too dumb to find the gate."

All rationale was gone. We were convinced we would be trapped inside. "What if someone on the job decided to close early because of the snow and locked us in?" I asked. Then we saw it, the break in the barbed wire. We sped to the car, where our driver was sound asleep, knocked on the window, and took the road back to the city.

Kraków was gray but warmer. A snowless afternoon stretched in front of us. We dragged ourselves through the city, not sure of ourselves or what our next step should be, until we heard the echoes of a quartet practicing. For once, I eagerly followed Melissa into a church. Strains of a viola pulled us in its direction as we gazed up and around, awed by the church's humble yet magnificent, brilliant-gold-flecked, cobalt blue ceilings. The art nouveau stained glass was vivid with twisting lilies. How could this beauty exist so close to the camps we had just visited? The juxtaposition was painfully disparate.

The strings continued to seduce us through the rooms until we found the musicians and sank down into a pew under another stained glass of gracefully entwined thorny roses. "Mozart?" I softly asked.

"I think so."

The music bounced off the windows and was absorbed by the wall's woodwork. The first violinist managed to bow skillfully, never once losing the vintage mink stole she smartly wore to keep her warm. We sat there for a very long time, bone- and blood-weary until we just had to go.

Back at our hotel, we were too weary to be more adventurous for dinner than walking downstairs. As we peered over the menu, I said, "I'm not writing about Belvedere, at least not in the way they would have hoped."

After what seemed like days of not eating, we had a simple plate of pasta that we had no right not to love. Wine was better in Kraków than in Warsaw, and we saw something completely unexpected on the list, like a mirage. There it was, as if it had been waiting for us, a wine from a little-known spot in the world, in the region of Italy's Alto Piemonte called Boca, from the remarkable grape nebbiolo. In Boca it was known by another name. The little area it came from had shrunk from several hundred acres to maybe twenty, but the vines still survived. Though it was delicious, and should have been savored, we drank it as if it were vodka, for courage.

## DRINK THIS

Santuvario
Vino Rosso
Grapes: Spanna, Croatina, Vespolina, Uva Rara
Where: Alto Piemonte, Italy

Raised in large Austrian oak casks in the garage next to Ivano and Paola's house on a busy intersection in Borgomanero, this is a typical blend for rossos; mostly spanna (the local name for nebbiolo), croatina, vespolina, and uva rara. The result is a stunner with lovely heirloom tomato and spicy herb with a pretty bouquet of thorny yet delicate American roses.

"That's Ivano's house," Diego said, pointing at a modern ranch with a wine tank in its driveway at the fork of two busy roads in Borgomanero. We were headed to Ivano's vineyards in the minuscule area of Boca, in Italy's Alto Piemonte region.

Diego Sorba's mother had pushed him to be a priest. That didn't work out. He became the landlord, as he referred to himself, of his quirky Parma wine bar, Enoteca Tabarro, where I first met him while researching in the Italian Emilia-Romagna region. During an evening of drinking and hanging out (Diego can talk), I was struck by his commitment to theater and tweedy Irish poets, and his intuitive way of understanding the soul of a vine. Whenever I visited, he left the bar, wife, and kids so we could take off to visit vineyards and people. In February 2020, when I was to be in Milan for a book signing, we had decided to spend the week before on a deep dive into alternative nebbiolo, the grape we bonded over. We weren't headed to Langhe, Piemonte's more famous area, home to Barolo and Barbaresco, but to the lower-rent zones, at upper Italy's frill, near the Swiss border. There the grape was often known by other names—picotendro, chiavennesca, and spanna—and blended with other grapes to round out the edge and rusticity.

I felt uneasy when I boarded the plane at JFK. My ninety-five-year-old mother was certifiably hysterical, convinced I would be infected by the mysterious virus currently spreading across the globe. Struck dead before landing. At the Malpensa Airport passport control, the officials scanned my temperature *Matrix*-style. As I waited for Diego, I got a call from the organizer of my event: "We're still on." I was relieved, but as I got into Diego's car, I had a premonition for the rest of the week when he said, "The wife just called. No school for the kids. Her work is shut down. I don't have to worry about my bar because bars are shut down." He shrugged and said, "Okay, then? Let's go."

And we did. After three days visiting vineyards closer to the Alps, we were headed east to Alto Piemonte and a small subregion called Boca where the grape was called spanna. This was a special area with special soils thanks to a geological disaster. The supervolcano, Valsesia, was active 280 million years ago; after about 10 million years of eruptions, the volcano imploded. The soils, crumbly poor granite, made for a very different expression for the local spanna. A deadly frost coupled with poverty after World War II robbed the region of its regal status, and farmers abandoned their land and fled to the cities. Those beautiful vines of spanna (and their blending companions, vespolina, croatina, and uva rara) became a rarity.

Diego gave me background on his friends whom I was about to meet. "Ivano played alto saxophone and repaired instruments. But he had a stroke almost twenty years ago and had to give it up. It was his partner, Paola, who urged him to prune his vines. She said that would be his therapy. It was."

I loved the notion of pruning as healing. There is a romance of pruning vines not just for the plant but for human physical and emotional strength. In more ways than one, the meditative effect of knowing where to make the most effective cuts on the vine to give it a long life is a rich symbol of vital force that continues no matter how traumatic. Survival. Life force. Healing.

We parked in the lot of a lumbering convent, Sanuvario (which influenced the name of their label, Santuvario). The couple approached; Paola, lean and tall, with bangs framing a finely boned and friendly face, had her arm looped through even taller, bearded Ivano's. As we walked into the vineyard, the friends chatted in Italian. Diego and Paola provided me with translations about how they'd cobbled together almost six acres of land, just the right amount for two people to handle on their own.

It was chilly, and we briskly hustled to see the Maggiorina, a historic vineyard where, hill after hill, vines are planted in the eponymous pruning style associated with it. Such an odd sight they were in that pre-spring moment, before the vines began to weep as they creaked back to life. The vines' arms looked like long spindly brown bones.

Ivano dug into the soil. "It has been a dry winter, the topsoil is dusty. But see? Below, it's moist," he said. I watched carefully as he clawed through the dirt. There were no signs of weakness from his past stroke. He stood up and as he explained the shape of the unusual trellising, he took two of the vines' long arms in his hands and moved with them. To me it was an eerily beautiful sight as if he was sensitively waltzing with skeletons.

Returning to the busy intersection where Diego had pointed out their house, we headed inside. We ended up taking our seats at the dining room table where, almost immediately, Diego retrieved the woolly salami he had cured in his wine bar's deep cellar, and he started to slice. Paola set out magnificently gooey cheese splattered with blue veins. Ivano prepared his wines. The table was littered with decanters and bottles. Each of his wines was dramatically different every year, showing not only the vintage but any trauma. The year

2016 must have been the most beautiful, because the expression made me want to sing.

Though I was taking care not to swallow, I was still getting buzzed and increasingly glad that I wasn't the one about to drive north, past Lake Como, in the darkness. Curious about how someone comes to make wine this way, I asked Ivano who had mentored him, and his answer surprised me. It wasn't some old, wizened local; it was a young, enthused Swiss, Christoph, an outsider who recognized greatness. Christoph was the first to make a public splash in upmarket wine magazines years ago when predicting the coming of age of Boca. It never came. "Christoph," Ivano said, "reinforced what my father had always told me: 'One must make a wine that resembles oneself.'" I couldn't figure out how old Ivano was—mid-fifties? Those blue eyes smiled with joyful melancholy. I looked at the man, then tasted again: Yes, the wine resembled him.

Diego paid for several cases of wines he needed for Tabarro. Paola and Ivano insisted we visit again soon, and we were off, stopping to fill up the gas tank and hit the Autostrada. Somewhere around Lake Garda, I received the news that all my events, book signings, and tastings had been canceled. Italy was headed into lockdown. "Oh well," I said. "So it goes."

It was a black night, and a howling frigid north wind was blowing off the early apricot blossoms. We talked of his kids, the wine bar, the world, the disease we knew almost nothing of, but we always circled back to the grape. "When I sip of the proper stuff, the important and expensive wines from Langhe, Barolo, and Barbaresco, those to me seem to carry the weight of responsibility of their greatness. On the contrary, whenever I drink the northern nebbiolos, like Ivano's, I feel uplifted and rather positively good-humored."

He put his foot on the gas because the young, earnest man who had made a wine from the chiavennasca grape in Valtellina, near the Swiss border, was making us dinner. Yes, we felt uplifted though the world was in chaos. The paradox did not escape us.

## Drink These Nebbiolos by Another Name

Mario Soldati, film director and writer of Italy's most famous wine book, *Vino al Vino*, said that seeing the vineyards of Carema was like seeing the skyscrapers of Manhattan for the first time. For me it was like that first time I turned around a corner and there, miraculously and breathtakingly, was the Forum. The sight of those Carema vineyards with their imposing Doric-like Columns perched right on top of the terrazzo-like terraces struck me as if Rome's Forum had been disassembled and splattered onto the mountainside. Dramatic, and so can be the wines. The city of Torino and industry lured young farmers from the must-be-a-mountaineer-to-farm-the-vines profession, and the land went to seed for decades. But history is being remade. The young and strong are coming back in search of great *terroir* that they can afford, while they are still fit enough to do the labor. Sipping the results, it's easy to realize that Soldati was right when he wrote, "Carema is strong and likeable as the sun and the stone." That is so true, but you can say that about all of these mountain nebbiolos.

The winemakers of the nebbiolo-growing regions in the Pre-Alps—Carema (in Piemonte), Alto Piemonte (in

Piemonte), and Valtellina (in Lombardia)—might or might not blend other grapes into the mix, but their nebbiolos (and the white erbaluce) are deserving of attention. Difficult to generalize but mostly the wines from the mountains are rugged with slightly tougher grit. Alto Piemonte is a bit rounder in the mouth and more to the blueberry. In Valtellina the hills are steep, and the calf muscles need to be powerful. Here the wines are a touch browner and with a more transparent taste, as if you can see through them. But no matter which region and expression, expect flecks of the nebbiolo that most of us know: licorice, rose petal, rusty nail, and tar with a touch of an angel's wings. These are wines that have bones, structure, and, well, a bit of humility. No matter where you pick, the wines are worthy.

Carema (picotendro):
Il Sorpasso,
Chiussuma, Ferrando, Muraje, Monte Maletto

Alto Piemonte (nebbiolo, spanna):
Odilio Antoniotti, Colombera & Garella, Santuvario,
Castello Conti, Francesco Brigatti

Valtellina (chiavennasca):
Alessio Magi, Le Strie, Arpepe, Dirupi, Barbacàn,
Pizzo Coca, Boffalora, Pietro Selva

# Dad's Last Gift

The crack of metal was like lightning. I whipped my head to see that, sure enough, Andrew had gotten into Dad's heavily secured file cabinet.

"Drumroll," I said. Now, I thought, we'd find it all out. Now we'd understand what kind of dramatic secret our dad had been harboring: the dead body, the woman, the child, the larceny, something, whatever it was, that had ruined his life. For decades we'd tried to analyze what went wrong and how someone so promising and charismatic could end up alone, broke, and having to quit his law practice before being disbarred. Andrew opened one drawer, then the other. "There's nothing in there," he said. "An empty treasure chest, a perfect metaphor for his life."

"But there is something there," I said, and reached in and tugged at what seemed to be a photograph.

Three weeks before, coming home from the blowing of the shofar that signaled the end of Yom Kippur, I was sitting down to break my fast, have some wine, and toast the new year when Andrew called. An hour behind in Milwaukee, he had just come home from shul.

"Dad is dead. He was found by a neighbor. Someone named Sharon." A woman, I thought. Of course.

I took a quick swig of the Jean Foillard Beaujolais, then stood up from the table, bumping into the wall on my way to the living room, my spatial sense completely lost. I was no longer hungry. "It's a joke, right?" I asked, clutching the phone to my ear. That a woman had found him wasn't surprising. That our father had died on Yom Kippur was. "Can you call Mom to tell her?" I asked.

"No," he said. "You."

"You," I insisted. "She'll take it better from you." Andrew, her son the doctor, was her favorite. I was too like my dad. I liked ritual more than religion, I was emotional, I liked my soup and my coffee blisteringly hot. I drank. She'd hear it more clearly from Andrew.

"Are you kidding? She's been waiting for all these years for widow status."

"It's more complicated than that," I said. "You know that."

He stopped kidding. "That's why you should do it. Anyway, I'll be doing everything else." Of course, it was true. He was going to ship Dad up to New York, take care of the documentation, the funeral arrangements. He was going to pay for it all; taking money from me wasn't an option.

So I called Mom, and she didn't miss a beat. Putting a voice to what Andrew and I merely thought, she said, "Death on the holiest day of the Jewish calendar was reserved for the holy, no? How did they let him in?"

They had been divorced for thirty-five years, rarely seeing each other except when they had to. Such was a time when we were staying at the same New Jersey hotel for his great-nephew's bar mitzvah. And yes, my mother was invited because that side of the family adored her. Bumping into each other at the check-in, Dad said, "We should have dinner tonight." My mother said sure. The last time they had dinner, she threw her drink in his face. I suspected I was to be on referee duty.

Dad ordered martinis all around. She went for the olive. He made a big show of taking out his insulin and his hypodermic. Before he drank, he stuck the needle in the gin to sterilize it. Mom stared as if to say, *Who is this jerk?* Then he jabbed himself with insulin in the gut, right there at the dinner table. At the end, he stuck us with the bill.

On our way back to the room, she leaned in to me and whispered, "What did I ever see in him?"

"Do you want me to tell you?" I asked her, but it was rhetorical. She'd rather think of herself as having been bewitched instead of hearing that he really was a movie-star-handsome charmer, was the extrovert to her introvert, and made her laugh.

"I should have seen through it," she said, reliving it all. "He terrified me from the beginning," she'd once told me. Interesting people always scared her.

Her father had tried to prevent the marriage. "Where do you come to someone like that who's not *frum*?" he yelled at her. My grandmother pleaded their case: "Shmuel, they are in love!" And he relented. When Dad came back from the war, they married, and he entered the law. They tried to change each other, and he even got her to go camping with him (there are home movies to prove it). The kids came, colleagues believed he was headed toward greatness, maybe even politics.

That damned religion thing, and like dipping the hypodermic into the gin, he loved to needle Mom about it. Thus the annual Day of Atonement fight. When the three of us were headed to shul, Dad, in short sleeves and shorts, would announce, "Meeting Bernie at the Grand Diner for a bacon breakfast!"

*Traif,* however, was the least of it. When the sexual revolution rolled around, he was the first to enlist, causing a whole level of grief for everyone involved.

What went wrong? This was the question that Andrew and I wanted answered, as if his path was as hereditary as his diabetes and we were in danger of following suit.

What went wrong? Did it start with Phyllis? Was it his passion for her that occluded his skill for law? Whatever reason, Dad started to lose case after case. He was desperate for money and yet held on to his seats at the opera long after he could afford them. After twenty years, Phyll and Phil split up and Dad confessed to me that she'd threatened murder-suicide if he didn't give her thirty-five thousand dollars as a palimony settlement.

The "nice" teacher he later married cleaned him of his household goods, and when he was recovering from back surgery, she took his house, his only equity. Packing up whatever was left, he fled to Tampa with the dog, "my girlfriend."

"But why there?" I'd asked. "You don't know anyone there."

"That's the point," he'd said.

I told my brother we had to admire him for at least being an optimistic depressive. At seventy-eight, he would reinvent himself.

A month after the funeral, Milwaukee-based brother and New York City–based sister rendezvoused in Tampa for the ritual disposal of Dad's belongings. I couldn't have been happier. It had been decades since Andrew and I had this kind of time together. It was Dad's last gift.

I was right behind my brother as he clicked the key in the lock to our father's garden apartment. Smells of dog hair and halitosis lit the air. In the Floridian heat and humidity, all bacterial activity accelerated, and bread was liquefying. Dishes were splayed like shale shards in the sink, covered with a furlike moldy coat. Maggots writhed over the garbage can. Except to take Dad to the morgue, no one had been in that flat for weeks. Pinching my nose with one hand, I propped open the window with my other. Then I pulled my hair into a ponytail. Andrew waved a surgical mask in my direction. "Put this on." Then he opened up a bag for me, and I pitched something into it that was stinky and unrecognizable.

When we had the kitchen under control, we pushed deeper into the apartment, in silence. This was nothing like my father's old shabby-chic 1930s ranch in the Hudson Valley, with the magnificent stone fireplace. Where was the past life of Philip T. Feiring? I wondered. Where does a life go? The messiness was familiar; his living room stereo was piled with vinyl records, Pavarotti and Sinatra. Photo albums were strewn about; the night of his death, he had been staring down his past. There was loose change on the table, and I noted Andrew sweeping quarters and dimes into his pocket. We inched toward the bedroom. Drawers open, clothes draped chairs, even the light had been left on. Andrew pointed to a depression in a soiled oatmeal-colored carpet next to the unmade bed. "He must have collapsed right here." He was quiet, almost reverential as he sank down on his knees and pressed his hand on the floor.

"Okay, Mouse," Andrew said, getting up, using my dad's nickname for me, "let's get to it." We took out the suit jackets, searching pockets. Andrew found coins everywhere. I saw him examine a handful of quarters as if they had some message for him from beyond—he had bailed Dad out to the tune of fifty thousand dollars a few years back. Dad owed him. Andrew again slipped the change into his back pocket, and we continued to fill plastic bags for Goodwill. "He was such a clothes horse," Andrew said, and it was not a compliment. Maybe that was why Andrew, even though a cardiologist, had an endearing lack of interest in material consumption.

One closet emptied. On to the dresser. We worked methodically. Maybe thirty minutes in, as if with telepathy, we wordlessly asked, Why are we pretending? He dropped the pile of clothes. We ran for the office. This was what we were really there for—the files.

After all these years, the old detective team was back on the job. As children in the sixties, as soon as our parents were out of the house and we were alone, we'd go directly to their bedroom and paw through Dad's underwear drawer, searching and sniffing for clues to find out when he was leaving and whom he was leaving for. Andrew took the closet, and I turned on Dad's old PC.

"I found something!" Andrew yelled out. He lugged the putty-colored metal filing cabinet that had been shrink-wrapped. The lock was so bound up with tape it seemed to be a plexi-bubble.

"Wow," I said. "The effort that took to secure it and ship it down. What did he want to keep secret?" I felt the excitement of a big reveal. This metal box had to be the time capsule that we were looking for.

Andrew found a box cutter and a crowbar in the toolbox. While he worked away, I prowled through computer files, desperate to find a hidden half-sibling, embezzlement, even the writings of remorse or those of a madman, so we could say, "He was nuts, what could he do?"

Andrew was getting frustrated with his project; the wrap was off, but he still couldn't get close to the lock. And I couldn't get into the emails without the password; however, I did see a file on that computer that said, "eHarmony"

"Uh-oh, Andy, I don't know how to tell you this."

He looked up at me.

"I have located the love file." I stared at it, my hand frozen in the air above the keyboard.

He put his hand over his eyes. "Please, no."

"You don't have a choice," I said. "I'm going in." I clicked and it opened. I looked at the dates. "He wrote them the night or day he died. Here you go. Ready?" I asked him. I had unhappily scanned the first email.

To Peg he wrote, "I will follow it up tomorrow. You really sound like hot stuff. Philip."

He never got to follow up.

To Lula he wrote, "I know how to please a woman, but we don't have to talk about it now."

And there was never a later.

Andrew sat cross-legged on the floor. "What a fuckup. His last night alive, with his dying breath, he was chasing women."

"What else would he do?" I asked with an icky feeling, as if I had just discovered his porn collection. Andrew saw only a man who walked out on responsibility. "He was lonely. Very."

Andrew didn't want to hear it, and he hacked away at the steel with force. "I'm getting it," he said.

I stood up, eager, and clapped my hands. "Bravo!"

And yet there was nothing.

We stared at a tinny void.

In that entire metal cabinet that Dad had shrink-wrapped, secured, locked three ways, and sent down to Florida.

"Wait," I said. "There is something."

My heart surgeon brother couldn't have been more precise as I extracted the photo. The paper was crinkled, but on the back I could read the date, 1947, and when I turned it over, I gasped. "You're not going to believe this." I handed it over to Andrew.

"Their honeymoon?" he asked me.

I nodded and saw our mother, looking like Myrna Loy, gazed into the camera, the palm trees in the back with serene blue water. She looked at him with such wonder, and she looked so soft and gorgeous. Only a man in love could have taken that photograph. No wonder when my mother heard of people getting divorced, she often said the same thing: "What happens to all of that beautiful love?"

Andrew and I focused on that snapshot of our mother for a long time. What was there to say?

Night had come. We hadn't eaten since a shitty morning whatever at Panera, where I complained bitterly and Andrew called me a snob. "There's somewhere I really want to go to for dinner," I said. My father's death was about the only thing that could have put me in Tampa, and I was not going to miss the legendary Bern's Steakhouse.

"Steakhouse?" he asked me. We were both vegetarians.

After a quick shower, we drove up to a bumpy-white-stucco-meets-strip-mall squat building. Andrew surveyed the place as if looking at a suspicious artery. "This?" he asked as a valet came by for the car.

Inside was a riot of burgundy and fringe bordello richness. "Dad would have loved this place," he said. "Especially
that waitress." He nodded at a woman of a certain age with
dangling earrings and false eyelashes. Once seated, Andrew
was presented with the wine list, which I grabbed from him,
shaking my head at the waiter's assumption. It was the size
of the *Gray's Anatomy.* Andrew looked on with amusement as
I gave it my full telescopic attention. "Those are all wines?"
He leaned forward with curiosity and asked, "What are you
looking for?"

"Something old and a bargain," I said, then I landed on a
1982 Jaboulet, Crozes-Hermitage, Domaine de Thalabert for
thirty-two dollars. "Stupid cheap."

"Unless it's crap," he said.

My nonexpert brother had been prophetic. The wine
was disappointing. "On its last legs," I pronounced of
the browned liquid. "But it is still interesting. Give it a
shot," I urged him, telling him how the fruit of youth had
changed into something more like sweet-smelling compost than a blueberry pie, but that wasn't so wrong. "This
wine is thirty years old, and it really would have been
great at its prime twenty years ago, but it still has something to say."

"Like what?"

"You can still taste the strength of the sun. It was a warm
year. But not high-acid, so it doesn't have as much life. You
can taste the transformation of the tannin—the tannic acid
that comes from the stems and seeds and grape skins; that's
the stuff that can make a wine taste rough or gravelly—into
something round, and if you listen to the wine very carefully,
you can taste just a hint of"—I searched for the word, it

was something like "honey" but not exactly—"almost sweet at the end. If only we all could age so gracefully." I shivered, thinking about those emails Dad had written.

"Why couldn't Dad have just told those women about his love of opera or photography, did he have to be so sexually inappropriate? It was completely demoralizing," I said, taking another sip.

"Because it was all he had left," my brother said.

"I suppose."

I remembered back to the couple of weeks beforehand; Dad's funeral. It was Andrew who wanted to speak. Searching for a positive memory, he seized on Dad's photography and home movies for the eulogy. "The documenter of the family," he had told the group of ten mourners. And in the middle of it all, his mouth quivered, and he struggled unsuccessfully to suck back the tears, which surprised me because he had such disdain for Dad. I had been worried he would take Dad's death poorly because there was so much unresolved. If there was hate, that meant somewhere there had been disappointed love.

"Andrew, are you okay? Being here. With everything? The safe, the letters, the death?"

"I'm fine," he said, and I didn't know if I believed him.

We were supposed to have two more nights to get through, but as we drove back to the comfortless Comfort Inn, even as I clung to every remaining second with my brother, I saw what we needed to do. Get out of there. "Andy, let's call a junk man. We don't need to go through every inch of crap."

He said, "Maybe."

In the morning, the light threaded through the blinds.

"Okay, Mouse," Andrew said to me. "Pack up and let's get the fuck out of here."

We were soon ready and waiting for Panera to open. I didn't complain about the coffee. Then we went off to the gated community.

We found a guy with a backward baseball cap and a truck. He came by, looked around at the clocks and the furniture, the clothes, everything. "I'll give you three hundred dollars."

Andrew said $350. The guy gave him the money and we were done.

Then we took one last look to see if we wanted to save anything. We took more than we thought: letters, stamp collections, most of the photographs, and the turntable. I took a picture of Dad and the dog, a vase that my aunt had given him, and a vintage, leather-bound Shakespeare collection that he'd always wanted me to have. And every time Andy saw more coins, he snatched them. We left the door open for the junk man and sped to the airport.

We got through security and happy to find we were going to fly from adjacent gates. Seeing a Starbucks, we ordered a couple of lattes. Andrew dug into all the pockets on his army fatigue jacket and measured out eight dollars in pennies, dimes, nickels, and quarters, and pushed them toward the tattooed and pierced young cashier. "To you from the estate of Philip T. Feiring. The T, our father always said, stood for *tuchas*."

She didn't crack a smile, but we laughed hard as we made our way to a table, giggling until tears formed. My belly hurt from laughing. Andrew took a sip and coughed it out, grabbed a napkin, and tried to stop laughing. "An empty safe!" he blurted out when he could finally talk again. I didn't remind him it was almost empty. Our laughter was redemptive. We had to laugh, otherwise it would be too much.

It seems as if I always cry on planes. There's something about the pressure that strips emotions bare. As the tears dropped, I put on my sunglasses for privacy and thought how my mother had been concerned about the money my brother had to shell out for the funeral. The day before the burial, she called me up and said, "It's only graveside, yet they want money for everything. Can you believe it? I'm taking over a tallis to Riverside. At least that will save your brother a hundred dollars."

"Whose tallis is it?" I asked.

"Your father's."

"My father had a tallis?"

She was so nonchalant, almost happy, when she said, "It's the one he wore at our wedding."

And so it came to pass that after my brother's fine speech about Phil the documenter, we took turns shoveling. I couldn't stop thinking how my mother had finally become a respectable widow, because under the pine, my father was wrapped not with a piece of Phyllis or Joyce or any other woman he was linked to, but in the prayer shawl he wore when he was still a young, charismatic guy with a future. What happens to all of that beautiful love? my mother asked. What happened was the same thing that happens to all potential: It is either fulfilled or not.

Clods of earth landed on top of my father's box. God, it seemed, wasn't the only one who had a handle on the ironic. My father was returned to both a religion and a woman he had loved yet denied. He would wear that tallis until it too crumbled to dust.

## DRINK THIS

Dard & Ribo
Crozes-Hermitage
Grape: Syrah
Where: Crozes-Hermitage, Northen Rhône, France

There's mystery, maybe a little fizz, horse dander, like sinew, like a sleek racehorse with muscle with punch, and silkiness, but yet also classic blueberry and animal and muscle and just that mystery that lurks under the crust. The last sip on this wine is truly the best, so cheat, and decant.

I like to think I'm vaccinated against hero worship. Yet I had to buttress my immunity to visit the notoriously standoffish Northern Rhône winemakers René-Jean Dard and François Ribo. When I first tasted their syrahs in the late nineties, my response was a double take so hard that I gave myself whiplash. I had never tasted anything like that from the North and immediately swore I'd visit the vineyard. The more I encountered those wines (mostly in Paris), the more I had to concede the two were gods of the winemaking kind.

Why is one drawn to one wine over another? What does it say about one's personality? Or, more specifically, my personality? I thought about the Northern Rhône's rugged landscape from which gorgeous syrah could be pressed. The region is not nearly as popular as Bordeaux or Burgundy, and that puzzles me. Oh, there are plenty of people grabbing the best bottles of Rhônes on the auction market; the greatness is recognized, but it's not an every-person people pleaser. Depending on the place, the grape may give savory more than sweet, muscle more than fruit, and bone more than fat. Some like more fruit, some like something gentler. Each to our own. I often visualize the wine's taste as sparks that fly when striking one rock against another, and I like that.

As Dard and Ribo spoke little English and my French is limited at best, I asked a local friend to attempt to schedule an appointment for me. I knew that the duo was famous for being reclusive and difficult. Why would they consider me so special? What hubris, I chastised myself. The friend told me, "I said you were a friend who was an American wine journalist. Ribo asked me what your last name was. I didn't know! That's when he hung up on me."

"You're kidding me, right?" I asked. "He actually hung up on you?"

Having other appointments in the area, I held my breath and drove down from Burgundy, where I had been, marveling at the landscape transforming from alabaster limestone to smoky granite. The Rhône region, south of the Beaujolais, west of the Alps, and just north of Provence, is a large, bisected region. The North and the South have little in common except a mighty river that runs through both, and they suffer the fierce winds that whoosh in from Africa. Differences? Those are more plentiful. Soils and grapes have little overlap. The South is lush; the North is angular. While Châteauneuf is the fanciest wine in the South, up North there's a string of a vineyard hierarchy, starting with Hermitage, Côte Rôtie, Cornas, Saint-Joseph, and Crozes-Hermitage. And steep? To visit many a vineyard, hiking shoes are needed. The southern grenache is mostly planted *en gobelet*, otherwise known as bush vines, and in the North, the musky red grape syrah is traditionally tied up, one vine per pole, and staked like giant tomato plants, called *échalas*.

There had been rumors of the syrah grape's origins in Shiraz, Persia, but those had been debunked by ampelographers, the field of botany dedicated to the grapevine. Indeed, those rocky soils surrounding the Northern Rhône area were home territory to this grape. Romans tended these vines, and it didn't take much of an imagination to sense the ancients amid the soil, the burning sun, and the punishing wind.

Until the twentieth century, the only place where the grape was grown outside the Rhône was in Australia. Some of Australia's oldest vines are syrah (they call it shiraz) in the Barossa Valley dating back to 1843. But for some reason, the grape has been a hard sell to Americans. More recently on the granite of southern Chile, the grape can rock. And yet, and yet, the Northern Rhône is just superior.

When I arrived in Tournon, I received word. The appointment was on! Delighted, I headed across the river, and at the post-lunch hour of two-thirty, I arrived at the Dard & Ribo winery in the appellation of Crozes-Hermitage.

The sun and heat were full throttle. The winery looked like a run-down barn in the middle of the Catskills, with all sorts of *schmutz* and broken-down farm equipment strewn around the grounds. At the side stood a clutch of old fruit trees. At the door, a black sign that had the letters "drrrinnngg!" was next to the buzzer. I *drrrannng*ed it, but no one answered. Fifteen minutes later, a truck drove up in a cloud of swirling dust, and François Ribo stepped out.

The winery was suitably messy. We commenced tasting, sampling barrel after barrel from various plots of Crozes-Hermitage, Saint-Joseph, and Hermitage.

Tasting was painful. While my hero worship faded as François talked to me in monosyllables, the aromas and flavors of the overlooked but gorgeous white roussannes spoke poetry. The syrahs? Oh, man. Olive, bacon, meat, blood, herbs, laurel, rosemary, and earth, cola without the sugar, something that I call horse sweat or horse dander, something powdery but with muscle, and some sort of big lift, like a ripe citrus. Coffee grounds? Or is that funk a touch of compost carried on sea air with energy. Give me that combo of sinew and pomegranate syrup, and it might as well be Prozac.

I had been trying to get a serious response from François for two hours. He kept ignoring me. I just couldn't stand the silence anymore and blurted out, "I love your wines. I am trying to find out something about you. I want to know how you can make wines this pure and expressive. What music do you listen to? What do you read? What do you drink?" This was not a high point in journalism. This was my one shot, and he was being so confounding! But the ice cracked and Ribo giggled, that "tee-hee" sort of thing. He answered in French I could well understand. "I love wine and also want to know the person who made it. I understand."

All right, then. I continued, "What do you like to read?" He actually answered me. He reads politics and nonfiction. He likes jazz.

I left with a bounce in my step as I reached the pebbled yard. Forgiveness bloomed in my heart. Maybe, like me and the wines of Crozes-Hermitage, he wasn't standoffish, merely shy.

### Drink These Syrahs

Is Hermitage better than Crozes or Cornas? Is Côte Rôtie better than Saint-Joseph? It depends, so decide for yourself. While I had a thirty-year-old Hermitage from the producer Jean-Louis Chave that made my knees weak, I get tremendous satisfaction from newer wines from Crozes and youngster wines from Cornas and St.-Jo. Côte Rôtie can be a little bit large for me, chunky, but from a few top producers like Texier and Jean-Michel-Stéphane? Well, more, please. The Northern Rhône is home territory and the undefeated champ, but as comparison, you need to discover those from other countries and think for yourself.

If you can't find Dard & Ribo, here are some of my other favorite wines from the Northern Rhône:

Thierry Allemand, Franck Balthazar, Mickaël Bourg, Domaine Auguste Clape, Domaine Pierre Gonon, Lionel Faury, Bernard Faurie, Alain Graillot, Domaine de l'Iserand, Domaine Lionnet, Domaine des Miquettes, Domaine Monier-Perréol, Philippe Pacalet (Burgundy but makes a delicious Cornas), Aymeric Paillard, Domaine Romaneaux-Destezet, Éric Texier

California: Hank Beckmeyer
(La Clarine Farm), Arnot-Roberts

Australia: Sam Vinciullo Winery, Harkham Wines, Shobbrook Wines

Chile: Macatho

Extra credit: There is very little white wine in the Northern Rhône. The flowery Viognier has its own regions, Condrieu, and the one domaine appellation, Château-Grillet. Saint-Péray, just under Cornas, is another white wine region; the grapes allowed there are marsanne and roussanne. But little bits of white with those grapes are also produced in Crozes-Hermitage, Saint-Joseph, and Hermitage. Dard & Ribo makes quite a bit with 30 percent of their production devoted to the (mostly) roussanne grape. Delicious, full-bodied, and satisfying. Look for theirs, Mickaël Bourg, Domaine Romaneaux-Destezet, Gonon, and Chave.

# TO FALL IN LOVE,

# DRINK THIS

Buzzed on an old Barolo made in the year I graduated college, I barely noticed the long haul up the stairs to my apartment. It was two in the morning, and I was warmed with the kind of emotional spark I hadn't felt with a man in way too long. Barolo, from northern Italy, a wine that can be licorice and berry in its youth and roses, peonies, and balsam with age, had always been the direct way to my heart, and maybe that's why I was musing over whether I had the nerve to jump back into the romantic world. I opened my apartment door oh so quietly—a friend of mine in from England hadn't been able to get a hotel room and was crashing with me for the night. An older gentleman, I gave him my bed. Anyway, I was sure he wouldn't fit on the couch as easily as I could.

He lay snoring away in an Ambien-fueled haze. I collapsed into the old chair in my kitchen. With lion's-paw arms, it was thronelike: It had been used as the "bride's chair" when my grandfather officiated at weddings. I unzipped my ankle boots, then tiptoed past the sleeping giant toward the water closet at the other end of the long apartment. I didn't put on the light, sat down, and could feel the pedestal wobble. Then I was like, What the hell? My feet sank into the oozing swamp of my eBay-bought Bokhara rug. I snapped out of my fantasies and reached up to a wooden bird attached to the light's chain. Water was everywhere. I looked up to the simple pine water box perched five feet above. It wasn't leaking. I looked at the toilet base. That was it. Damn. Gordon was such a big fellow, at least six-four; his weight must have been too much for the plaster that kept the toilet in place, so it was lopsidedly perched precariously on whatever was below. My apartment was so fragile, it easily broke, as if it had osteoporosis.

This was not the kind of situation I could deal with at two-thirty in the morning, but I sopped up the mess and wrote a note: "Don't flush!" I made up the couch and didn't sleep a wink.

In the morning I heard Gordon make his way to the toilet. "Don't flush!" I yelled. "What we have in there is a situation." I explained the disaster to him and went to put the coffee on.

"Alice blue gown," he said after he was dressed and ready to go, not even wanting to have breakfast with me, "I'm too old to walk these stairs anyway. I'm staying with another friend who has a working toilet and a real shower." Then he apologized, gave me a hug, and was gone. Meanwhile, I called my landlord. "Emergency situation."

Around eleven a.m., Mr. Plumber trudged up the steps. When he reached the fifth floor, I saw a pleasant-looking man in a Yankees baseball hat, short, solid, and probably two decades my junior. "My savior!" I cried.

He was not impressed with his hero's reception, and as he huffed, he muttered something about being out of shape. He would not lift his eyes to mine. Professionally, he asked to see the patient, my bathroom.

He entered through my kitchen and glanced to the tub that was adjacent to my sink. In my railroad apartment, a string of open rooms, my whole life was exposed to anyone who wandered through, and the plumber was taking it all in: where I bathed, where I slept, where I worked. We proceeded through my bedroom, into my study and living room, and at the far end of the apartment, near the street, I pointed to the patient. I watched as he looked up at the elevated water tank and its pull chain. He examined the fragile copper pipes and pulled the chain as I cried out, "No!"

Sure enough, like the Trevi fountain, water poured and spouted from everywhere. Shit, I thought, what kind of plumber can't see that he shouldn't have flushed?

"Oh, fuck me!" he exclaimed, slapping his palm against the wall. "Miss, this is an old toilet." Clearly, working on a museum piece was not his idea of a good time.

"Yes, I know." I was terrified he was going to tell me that he was headed to Home Depot to bring me up to modern times. I felt that if I had to have a standard-issue flush toilet, my heart would break again. He had no idea how emotionally attached I was to my porcelain convenience.

He took it all in. He looked at his project and asked, "Who built that water tank for you? It's beautiful. But not original."

I gazed at the perfectly dovetailed Siberian-pine water box. "My old boyfriend." Ronny was a good fixer. When the original box sprang leaks, he made us a new one.

I saw the plumber register the "old." "Why did you let him go?" he asked. "Someone makes you something like that, you keep him."

This was a guy used to having his heart broken instead of the other way around, I noted.

About to head out to buy supplies, he saw my wall of wine and flinched. "Holy crap," he said. "Miss, you drink a lot or what?"

"I'm a wine writer."

His eyes bulged, and he let out a snort of laughter. "I know people drink wine," he said, "but what's there to write about?"

"Their stories," I said.

He shook his head with amazement, as if I'd told him I had a talking frog. He found it even more hysterical when I said, "I don't have enough wine."

"How many bottles?" he asked.

"*Hmm,* about a hundred and seventy? I want about two thousand."

He then scanned the disorder that marked my work area. "You some sort of artist girl? I mean, you know, an artist does her own thing, and I'm looking around here and, you know, the lamps, the colors, that crazy desk you work at, you do your own thing." He walked over to a few watercolors on the wall. "You do these?"

"Yes."

"See? I was right." He was pleased with himself. "You play that violin?"

"Sometimes."

Over the next three hours, the inquisitive plumber soldered, anchored, cursed, talked to himself, patched, made a complete mess, ruined my best towels, and traipsed plaster over my floorboards and rugs. Taking breaks from the toilet drama, he ventured out to see if I was still pounding the computer keyboard, to look over the wines again, and to find other evidence of the work the old boyfriend had done. "Did he make your desk?"

"Yes."

Another rueful shake of the head. I knew exactly what he was thinking.

"Look at that," he said, noting the curvy shape of one of the desk flanks. "You got to take him back, miss. " He toured the rooms. "He do this?" he asked, gesturing at the ornate iron welding on one window that Ronny had made to keep me safe at a time when my block was more dangerous.

"Yes."

"He rebuilt your floors? Did he build those shelves the wines are on?"

I nodded.

"And you let him go? Why did you let him go?"

What to tell him? Finally I said, a little annoyed, "I really didn't have a choice in the matter."

He reacted as if he'd been told of a death. And I realized he had his own stories. I saw what he was seeing—the love, the attention, and the thought that had gone into every piece of construction in my apartment. "I'm sorry too, " I said.

"Sorry, miss. Sorry I asked."

He went back to his work, taking a break from time to time to talk. This romance thing was bugging him. "I don't have luck with girls either," he complained. I took umbrage—I never thought that I didn't have luck with men—but he wanted to talk, and I was curious where he was going, so I said, "Really?"

"There was one, she was old, about forty-eight"—Jesus, I thought, I was the other side of fifty myself, I was ancient—"she lived down in Puerto Rico. She made money; she was a teacher. We were talking about 9/11, and I told her I was there when it happened. I told her I could have been killed. Do you know what she said? She said, 'It was a good thing the towers went down, America learned a lesson.' I couldn't look at her after she said that. I can't deal with crazy shit like that."

He hit his palm with his large wrench, shaking his head, biting his lip, then continued.

"My old girlfriend? I mean old." He chuckled. "I guess I like older women."

I buttoned the top button of my blouse.

"She dumped me, but a few months ago, she rang the doorbell and said, 'I haven't seen you in a long time. I want you.' We have sex. After, she walked around my apartment as if she owned the place and told me what I could and could not do and the way it's going to be. Women just like to control you. That was it. I threw her out. Good riddance." Then he gave me advice: "Don't control your man."

Thanks, I thought. I'll try to remember that.

He replaced the sputtering, leaking copper pipe with gleaming stainless. That hurt, to see the copper go, but what could I do? The dusky smell of solder filled the apartment. He cemented the toilet bowl back into place, saying, "This was never put in right."

"Yes, I know. Sewer gas always leaked out of it."

"It sure did. It stank in there."

It's odd, so few people ever noticed those fumes. It was Ronny who first identified the occasional smell from the faulty installation—one of the few things he didn't fix before he left.

"The toilet is in!" my plumber finally announced after what seemed to be far, far too long. "It won't smell anymore or move when you sit on it. Go ahead. Push it. Try it. You can't budge it."

When I first met Ronny, he challenged me in a manner of flirting more appropriate of a sixteen-year-old than a man of thirty-two. We were on the porch at a mutual friend's house in the country, I thought trying to fight our outsize attraction for each other. "Punch my stomach," he said to me. He was long-boned and lean. "It's like iron. Go ahead. Hard. It won't budge; you can't hurt me. Go ahead."

Ronny and I luxuriated in love for eleven years, yet the ending was the opposite, razorlike and quick. As I return home from visiting vineyards in Sicily, having sensed there was something wrong, I spent hours on the plane crying. I was prepared to tell my beloved Mr. Fix-It that there was something terribly wrong between us and I wanted us right again. Our relationship needed the attention he gave to the apartment. As it turned out, he felt this wrongness too but had another solution.

He carried my bags up the five flights and then, once inside, led me to the plain pine bench he had made for me. There, as if I were already sitting shiva, he told me he had to leave.

Leave? But I just got home. What do you mean, leave?

Over the years during which Ronny turned my chicken coop into a rustic palace, I had told him one of my many fears: "You're like a cat marking property. You're leaving your smell everywhere. And if you leave, how would another man ever be here with me?"

I was not into Mr. Plumber, and hopefully he wasn't into me, but he sensed Ronny's mark. As I returned to my computer, the man began to pack up his tools, and I wondered if by repairing my bathroom so thoroughly he was trying to show that my old love wasn't the only one who could fix what was broken. It was a lesson worth listening to. I owed him for that. And for fixing my leak.

I got a big fat idea. "What kind of wine do you like?"

"I don't know, but I don't like them really dry."

Most people say they like dry, but they drink sweet. I didn't know if I could trust he was telling me the truth.

"I do like them cold. Which ones do you drink cold?"

"White or pink," I told him. I was about to tell him that some light reds as well can take the chill, but that seemed like Wine 2.0. As if he'd heard me, he said, "I don't really know anything about wine, but I would like to."

I looked at what I had on hand that I could give away; with little experience, would he really appreciate the quirkier wines I had to offer? I would feel guilty if I handed off some of the generic, boring (yet free) samples that wineries often sent to me back then. He deserved better than that. I had this crazy thought that if I offered him the right wines, I could change his luck with women and if I was going to be successful, I had to give him some good stuff.

After five hours of getting to know this man, of seeing how observant he was, of listening to his commentary on race, women, politics, and what it meant to be Puerto Rican, of hearing how he didn't really speak Spanish, just enough to pick up girls, I thought I had enough info to make my choices.

Feeling as if I were reading his tarot, I reached for a California chardonnay—I'm a little embarrassed about this because it was a wine that I never would have liked, all vanilla-scented and gloopy. I told him to drink it super cold with someone who liked the obvious.

Next I chose a Spanish albariño. He liked that. "Some of my relatives were from Spain," he said. "Not sure where."

"Well, this one is from Galicia, on the northwestern shore of the Atlantic, not far from Portugal. Most are really commercial, but this one is the real thing. It comes from crusty granitic soils and is made with a lot of respect. Open this one with someone who has potential for the long term," I said. "If she likes it, that means she's a thinker who won't try to control you. You should consider her for another date and maybe more." Finally, I handed him a bottle of Moscato d'Asti. "Look, there's a lot of bad wine like this on the market, I see it all the time. Orthodox Jews who love sweet wine think a Moscato is delicious, like, you know the one in the blue bottle?"

He shook his head, no.

"Terrible stuff. This one is gorgeous. This is not for a first date. Maybe the one who hated the chardonnay or thought the albariño was interesting, maybe you'll go here for that second date. At the beginning of the evening: After all, it's only a half-bottle. Make it super cold. Prepare her for a little sweetness but fizz and power and tart; if she laughs because the wine is surprising, then that's it. That's the one."

He was my new best friend. "This one?" he asked. "The sweet one?"

"Yes! But not really too sweet." I was starting to believe my own spin, yet I wanted to communicate to him that from my point of view, people didn't need to see taste the same way. My intention was to suggest that where tastes diverge and overlap were worth listening to. After all, someone who has no toler-ance for fiery spices can be happily in love with someone in the hotter-the-better camp. A vegan could be mad about a steak lover. It depends on what kind of love and intimacy one looks for. And, if I could lead him out of his disappointment with women with the help of a bottle, well, that was the best tip in the world. But just in case, I handed him a twenty.

"Miss, I can't believe you're doing this. Man, these are lucky charms," he said, gathering the wines in his arms, a great big beaming smile on his face. But I was indebted to him, the man who'd saved my toilet. I felt that he took the bottles as I gave them to him, with hope for his future.

The man had been in my apartment since eleven, and it was now closing in on five. I finally asked him for his name.

"Juan," he said, pumping my hand.

"Alice," I said.

"And the sweet one, this is the one?" he said, holding up the bottle. "Even its shape is sexy."

"Yes, that's the one."

He stuck his bottles in his plumber bag; he was at the door and leaving. Then he turned around and asked, "What did your old boyfriend drink, the one who did all the work?"

I told him that would have to wait for the next plumb-ing emergency because it was a long story. After he left, just for fun, I went to flush the toilet, then I went to my computer and emailed the man from the night before with whom I drank the somewhat faded roses of the Barolo. No longer should my apartment or my love life serve as a mu-seum piece.

## DRINK THIS

Nanclares y Prieto
Dandelion
Grape: Albariño
Where: Rías Baixas, Galicia, Spain

This wine comes from the granitic soils of Cambados on the Atlantic, where Alberto Nanclares is one of the few (but growing) farmers and winemakers working naturally. Here the wines are as they should be. High in acid, naturally made. Sophisticated. Lemongrass hints. Power. Grace. Note: The bottle lasts forever once open.

"Swim past the ropes with me": That's what Ronny wrote on my lined reporter's notebook, under the light of the candles flaming in a friend's country kitchen sometime before dawn.

The notion terrified me. Not that I couldn't swim, but that I was being encouraged to swim past safety. In wine, sure; in life? I'm all for testing, but did I really want my heart hammered?

Ronny was thirty-two when we met. He drank St. Pauli and Guinness, drank margaritas with fresh lime juice, and he was also very proud of buying Mouton Cadet by the caseload from Costco. Some people think they can change a future mate's clothing style; I used to think I could influence their drinking. Mouton Cadet was, and is, a very popular generic Bordeaux that benefits by its association with the grand and mighty Mouton Rothschild, one of Bordeaux's most expensive and revered wines. The way to think of Cadet, which refers to "Junior," would be if the fancy Cadillac company produced the junky Yugo. The wine is from bought grapes, made in a fashion that I'm not even going to guess, costs about twelve dollars a bottle. A friend of mine wisely called it "wine as punishment."

Ronny loved good food. He was attached to superior ingredients. He (famously and obnoxiously) went through friends' spice cabinets and threw out the ones that had outlived their usefulness. He smelled their oils to protect them from rancidity. We had the nose thing in common. There was no way I could allow him to believe Mouton was superior. If he liked it, fine. But he had to like it armed with knowledge. In our budding relationship, Ronny was not convinced that I could lead him places. The only way I could possibly manage to move his taste odometer was by showing, not telling.

As was my habit. I invited about eighteen friends to an

evening soirée. I cooked for days, roasted this and that, vegetarian liver, potato tortillas, and olives. Cheese. Yes. Especially smoky mozzarella from (the now sadly defunct) Joe's on Sullivan. I wrapped up fifteen bottles in white paper and, with a fat Sharpie, numbered them. The commonalities in the wines were their location and color—Western France and red. My guests were asked to decide which ones they liked. Which they hated. Write descriptions if they were so inclined. The time came, and I unveiled each bottle to shock and awe.

My beau had been convinced that number three was the worst of the lot, and it had won his most venomous description: "gasoline mixed with squirrel droppings." It was the Mouton Cadet. He never went back.

Over the next decade, his tastes blossomed. He liked the ones with a little sweetness; he loved muscats, especially the one I had given Juan, Bera Moscato d'Asti, one of the few organic and authentic ones. He loved savory wine, didn't really "get" Burgundy, but whoa, did he have a taste for champagne. It took him a while to warm up to Barolo, but eventually when he saw me take one out, he genuflected. However, if there was one wine of our relationship, it was the violet-scented, chalky-textured wine from the Loire Valley, from the now-defunct Clos Roche Blanche. Juan had told me not to control "my man," and you shouldn't control anyone, but providing guidance was another matter.

Because wine preference should not be limited to color, I tried to get Ronny to explore white, which for some reason seemed anti-macho. My tutelage began with a riesling that had some residual sweetness (breakfast wine, he declared). Finally, it was wine from the Atlantic that did it for him.

The Atlantic is the earth's second largest body of water

and the world's saltiest sea. The climatic influences include clouds, rain, humidity. There's also mildness and that translates into longer growing seasons. Get out your map. Atlantic wines can include Long Island, western coastal Loire (muscadet!), the northern stretch of Spain, Galicia, the northern side of Tenerife, Rías Baixas, Jerez, parts of Portugal (such as the other side of Galicia, the Minho province that produces Vinho Verde), Maine, Prince Edward Island, and Nova Scotia (hello, global warming, coming to a bottle near you soon). Those white wines can be razor-sharp, bright, edgy, rarely anything but super dry, almost neutral, but with a grip and creaminess like sea foam. Real albariños, like the one offered by Nanclares, have become so rare that you want to suck them all down when you find them.

Alberto Nanclares was once an economist. In 1993 he moved to Rías Baixas, where albariño comes from, a land of pink-quartz-flecked granitic soils, to be near the sea and indulge his love for boating. The house he bought was in Val do Salnés and came with vines. The vines stared at him. He stared back. Nanclares slowly gave in to the plants that would soon overtake his life. At first he used chemicals, but he quickly realized his folly and stopped. He initially made wine with an enologist. Old-fashioned albariño was a refreshing wine with a tasty saltiness. The aromatics are subtle; the wine's charm comes from a lemony acidity and an edgy thrill. But the enologist encouraged him to make it in a way that had become popular: Basically, the choice was either turn it into a sauvignon blanc or a riesling look-alike and reduce the acid, as marketers had determined that a wine that said "zing" was too much for the general drinking public. In other words, the smart grape got dumbed down. Dismayed by the wine he was making, Nanclares said, "To hell with you," and kept his natural acids. After that, he made wine on his own.

Drive around the area and you'll see granite poles supporting old vines in pergola training, where the vines create a netting overhead, high above the grass below. This old-fashioned training is actually wisdom and keeps the grapes safe from the constant threat of mildew from the humidity. Up high, they can dry out in the Atlantic winds.

Like muscadet (from the melon grape) in the western Loire, the wines have a delicious salinity, and as with muscadet, it's best to vinify them simply. Unlike muscadet, where fermentation often happens in old concrete vats, the best wines here are likely made in old, large, and neutral oak barrels that do not (or should not) impart any taste but round out the angles of this high-acid wine.

In the end, Ronny chose to go back to Mouton Cadet, not for real, let's just say metaphorically. Anyway, by nature, he's more of an ale person. I suppose while we were together, we swam past the ropes of safety in our own way. If you're the kind of person who's looking for a kind of romantic love, and a possible partner tries to seduce you to swim past the ropes of emotional safety with them, I advise you not to unless you're committed to drama. Or at least know how to swim in the Atlantic. But better you find someone who can drink from its shores instead.

## DRINK THESE ALBARIÑOS

A tiny bit of albariño is grown in California, with decent results, but nowhere other than Rías Baixas will you get the edge of the northern coast of Iberia. Because it could well be considered a neutral grape—much like muscadet. But left to its own devices, albariño's true nature can take on notes of linden and gentle spring flowers in the distance, and these only get more profound with a little age. To put these gorgeous wines into new oak is a sin; best to have absolutely no taste influence. Again, like the Muscadet, they're best vinified and raised in cement or old wood or even clay. Unfortunately, there aren't a lot of them; however, there are some spectacular whites from Rías Baixas farther inland, not albariño, but from the worthy doña blanca and godello.

Rías Baixas, Spain: Adega do Vimbio, Bodegas Albamar, Nanclares y Prieto, Adega Entre os Ríos, Lagar de Pintos, Pedralonga, Do Ferreiro

And in the United States it's a whole different thing:
Swick Wines (Oregon), La Clarine Farm (Sierra Nevada Foothills, California), Southhold Farm and Cellar Cup (Texas!)

# OPERATION ETHEL

When a superstorm came rolling up the East Coast, Ethel was a few weeks shy of her eighty-eighth birthday. Powered by some hardwired circadian rhythm, she had continued to commute via car to her Bowery jewelry exchange kiosk from Long Beach, Long Island. It was something she'd done for more than forty years. Ever since the divorce, selling glittery stuff—diamonds and the rest, antiques, and engagement rings, something she detested at the beginning—had been her life force. Depending on traffic, the round trip could take five hours, a hardship that has driven far younger merchants to public transportation. "Can't keep a good woman down," she explained when people looked at her like someone out of Ripley's. But just because she's independent and feisty didn't make it any easier for me when she, who lives a block from the beach and a few more from the bay, refused to displace herself because of a lame hurricane named Sandy. I pleaded with her, "Come to me in New York. Humor me. We'll have fun."

Her feet had grown roots. She wasn't going anywhere. I really wanted to be a dutiful daughter, but she sure didn't make it easy.

The night when the wind whipped up and sent the plants on my fire escape flying, I checked in on her as often as I could while I could. "You okay?" I asked after the lights went out in New York City. Long Beach had already been in the dark for hours.

"I walked into the wall," she said, laughing.

"Didn't you have a flashlight?"

"It was in my hand," she answered.

"It wasn't on?"

"I didn't think I needed it."

That's when the phone went dead.

When I laid my head on my pillow, I kept on fretting over why she was so damned stubborn. If anyone was going to ask me her secrets for longevity, it would be superhuman ability for denial and fierce loyalty to intractability.

The next morning, the sun flooded through the window, waking up my anxiety. In my NoLita neighborhood, the morning was silent and cold. Like a good Luddite, I still owned a nondigital phone and a landline, so even with a dead iPhone, I could have some connectivity. My cousin Judi was hysterical: "What is the matter with her! She could have come here, to me!" My brother had been diagnosed with pancreatic cancer just two months before the storm. He was deep in chemo fog and yelled at me from Milwaukee, "How could you let her stay there?"

As if it were my fault? I told him, "Judi asked her. Sarah offered her apartment near the UN. She could have come here. But you know what she's like." I choked up and held the phone away so he couldn't hear me. What was I going to do without him. I got my voice back and said softly, "Andy, you're the only one she listens to, you know that."

"I know," he said. "But what can I do?" He was resigned to dying.

While the world might have seen Ethel as strong and heroic at work, an independent divorcée who should have been the star of her own sitcom, burrowing down in Long Beach during Sandy wasn't so much about her bravery as her systemic fear of action.

When she downsized from split-level to the receptacle for the homeless and insane that Long Beach was in 1976, she explained, "It's temporary." She unpacked thirty years later.

Suggest she get on a plane, train, or subway by herself and she'll turn agoraphobic; put her behind the wheel of her Corolla, she's Fearless Fosdick.

Fearless or not, I needed to find her, and so in order to do that, I needed to find a connection to the Internet. I was just about to launch my newsletter—my latest attempt to make a living—so I called my friend Okey, who was designing the site. When he picked up in the office, I was ecstatic. "Wow! You have power!"

"Come on up!"

With the subways out of commission, I ran up to Twenty-seventh Street as fast as I could. Along the way, I saw people holding power cords, like vampires looking for electrical blood. I got to the On Design office and hopped on a computer, opened the Google bar, and typed in "Long Beach."

There it was. As bad as New York City was, Long Beach was worse. No water. No cars. No homes. What they did have was a state of emergency. The National Guard was to move in the following day. The wild imagination my mother had always accused me of was going wild. My mother hadn't been delusional when she said the water almost reached her terrace. She was swept away to the ocean. She was smothered by seaweed. She died alone in bed after giving herself a concussion. She got into her car during the storm and drowned. Or she was balled up under the covers, terrified. I had to get to her before the troops did. My mother, who wouldn't even undress in front of a doctor, would never survive a night in a displaced-persons shelter—that is, if she was alive.

Simultaneously, I gave approval to send the Hurricane Sandy Edition of the inaugural edition of *The Feiring Line* into the universe and posted a dramatic message to Facebook: "Anyone have a car to lend me to help me find a missing mom?"

The miracle of social media. Within seconds, an old friend was calling me. "I'm coming to get you."

"Perfect."

Ozzie was an actor turned math teacher and an old friend of my ex. Ronny eventually left, but Oz, a friend forever, stayed. He picked me up in his Subaru with a big smile that spoke of adventure. "Operation Ethel, let's go!"

He didn't know that phrase had been used for a different mission. Once we were over the Williamsburg Bridge, I told him. "At the beginning of September, Andrew was supposed to fly in on a Friday for a family wedding. It was a rare treat, as he mostly stayed away from family functions. I had canceled everything in my calendar so he and I could spend as much time together as we could. At about ten in the morning, I was surprised to get a call from him. 'You here already?' I asked. I was so lighthearted and then realized everything was wrong. He said, 'I'm at the hospital. Getting a chemo pump. Pancreatic.'

"Oz, we had the arrogance that comes from no cancer in the family. These things did not happen to us."

I paused, reliving and remembering. It was still so fresh. Andrew said if he was not lucky, he had a month. If he was, he had a year. Doctors are the worst. They know the statistics. As far as he was concerned, he was done. "Andrew, couldn't you get lymphoma? Kidney? You have to go and get fucking pancreatic cancer?" I asked.

"Well, if you're going to get cancer, you might as well go all the way."

That was the way we were with each other.

You cannot leave me alone, I remember thinking. We had too much to go through together, and I already missed him so much ever since he moved to Central Standard Time. He was too young at sixty-one, and couldn't die on me. But yet the higher powers hadn't bothered to ask my permission.

"We had to deal with Mom. We did what we did well together. Plotted. Operation Ethel. See? This is the second one. How to tell Ethel that Andrew is going to die? How do you do that?" I asked Oz.

I remembered how I packed a small bag—of course, wine, because I was going to need more than Mom's shit Shabbos wine to get me through the next two nights I would be staying with her. "I took two bottles." Two in case one was corked (the term used to describe a cork infected by the 2,4,6-trichloroanisole compound in bacteria, which makes a bottle smell and taste like a moldy basement).

I timed my train to get to Long Beach a few minutes after her commute back home. Like a spy, I watched her enter the building at five p.m. "She'll be in the apartment in five minutes," I texted Andrew. I waited fifteen minutes, then I waited at the door, my ear pressed against it. No screaming. He pinged me: "Finished." I let myself in with my key.

"Oz," I said, "I watched her try to cope with the news. She was talking to herself, repeating, 'This is not happening, this is not happening.' Hours later, well after midnight, she was sitting and talking to herself at the kitchen table. I sat down, took her hand, and she told me a story. 'When Andrew was four years old, he was very sick, he had a very high fever, and I was sitting by his bed, very worried. He said, 'Go to sleep, Mommy, I'll be okay.'"

The Long Island Expressway was so empty we could have had a picnic on it. "The wrong child is dying," I said.

"Come on, Alice," Oz said. He didn't like such talk.

By the time we hit Lido Boulevard in Oceanside, the scene was postapocalyptic. There were no floods, but there was evidence of the ocean and bay colliding. There were no operational traffic lights. Boats and cars were facing wrong directions and piled on top of Nathan's Clam House; power lines were scattered as if the wind had played pick-up sticks. After the Long Beach Bridge, refugees, looking like they were out of some war film, walked north, trailing suitcases, holding paper bags, vacating before the night fell. In the middle of E. Park Avenue, cars were covered with sand dunes.

The sun was fading, Long Beach looked grainy. On Maple Boulevard, the higgledy-piggledy cars were seaweed-draped and sand-swept. The grand Lido Beach Hotel, the former edifice everyone had referred to as the "Pink" Hotel's proud stone wall had been breached. My mother's building was boarded up. "You wait here," I said to Oz, and I ran out of the car, stood in front of where the front door used to be, and shouted up to the terrace, "Ethel!" No peeking through the curtains. No creak of the door. It wasn't looking good. I didn't have keys to her apartment. I was flunking daughterhood. How was I going to get in that place? By a miracle. And that was when someone running from the building let me in. I glided up the stairs and pounded on her door. There was nothing. Then I pounded the door with my open hand, yelling her name.

Behold. Tentative steps. She opened the door, and the waxy smell of freshly lit candles darkened the air behind her. She looked smaller than usual, as if she had shrunk to hobbit size overnight. The light was waning through the old curtains like a halo over the plants on the neglected baby grand, with ivories curled like toenails on a cadaver. Mom was backlit, looking fragile, and that black, blue, and yellow bruise over her sparkling green left eye from walking into the wall was stunning. My usually tactile-defensive mother threw her arms around me. I realized that for all of her bravado, she was terrified. "My hero."

"Pack. I'm taking you out of here," I said, as if I had ridden into town on a white steed.

"Don't be silly," she said. "I'm not going anywhere."

"Do you think I'm here for dinner?" I asked her with every drop of irony.

She actually did think that I had come to stay and tough it out with her, not to put her into a car and deliver her to light and warmth.

"Come on. Get your things together," I said, bossing her around for the first time in my life.

She ignored me and told me, "My car's dead." Then she put on a comic face of mourning. Just like my mother. She thought she was the only one.

"You're in excellent company. So is everyone's in this town and in Far Rockaway and just about everywhere near the water. Come on. Please. Pack," I repeated, feeling the coming curfew. I couldn't trap Ozzie out there away from his wife, in a place where there was no wine or flushable toilet.

"Did you know they are expecting looting?" she said.

"How do you even know that?"

"Diane looked in on me and gave me some news."

This was the first time, to my knowledge, that my mother had talked to anyone in the building. Progress. "I'm glad to hear it. Come on. It's getting late. Let's go."

"I can't," she said, then thought of a more appropriate answer. "I don't want to go."

"Stop being a child. You have to."

"Don't tell me what to do, you have the roles reversed here." She's such a pain in the ass, but sometimes she's awfully cute.

"Where would I go, to your place?"

"I don't have electricity either. Judi's," I said. "She really wants you to come. You'll be very comfortable there."

"She has a cat."

"You can put up with the cat."

"I don't like cats."

We were at a standoff. "Pretend it's a dog," I snapped.

She batted her eyelashes at me, and then it occurred to her that my arrival had taken some effort, that I didn't have a car. Of course, because she had no electricity and no smartphone, she had no idea what was going on in the rest of the world. She didn't know how bad it was out there. She didn't know about the thousands of homes lost, about the town's curfew, about the lack of public transportation. "How did you get here? The train?" she asked.

I explained there was no public transportation pretty much anywhere. "A friend drove me."

She narrowed her eyes as if to yell, as if he were another disagreeable beau, and then she quizzed, "Who is he?"

"A friend."

"And I never heard of him?" She pressed her car keys to me. "Is he Jewish?"

"He's my friend."

"So, he's not Jewish." She paused for a second, shook her head as if to say, *What am I going to do with you,* then said, "Have him take a look at the car." She then foraged in her large sack of a bag where she kept her life. She finally found the keys and I took them from her.

"Ozzie and I will take a look. But when I come back, please be ready. Okay?"

There are few things funnier than when a little old lady flips you the finger in the middle of a disaster. I wasn't going to waste energy getting angry. I had vowed to protect her. A thick husk had grown around her heart, but she was still a mother about to lose her son. Now she was my responsibility. I skipped down the steps and found Ozzie standing in front of the building. "Let's go check out her car," I said.

We walked down on Maple Boulevard, toward its bay

side to the parking lot. There were about fifteen cars that would never start again. All of them were wearing shrouds of bright green sea lettuces and brownish knobby rockweeds. Many were piled under sand. But my mother's Corolla was shiny. She'd obviously spent the day after the storm washing off the sea's schmutz with paper towels and, from what I could smell, Windex. Inside, the story of the night was illuminated. The interior was soaked, and it reeked of salt water and gasoline.

"It's done for," Ozzie proclaimed. On the walk back for Ethel, we detoured through the flattened walls of the now abandoned hotel moved several feet from its foundation. We stood, stunned by the force of the water and its damage.

She was waiting. "That's all?" I asked, peering into the paper bag that doubled as luggage. Mom was taking a towel and a pair of underwear and a few toiletries. "You realize you're not just going overnight? They have no idea when Long Beach will be habitable."

"Oh, I'm coming back," she said.

I didn't push. She could buy whatever she needed in Queens where Judi lived, where stores were open and there was warmth, electricity, and water. The point was to get her out of there while she was still willing. By some miracle, we managed.

She got into the backseat of the Subaru. She had an air of excitement about her, as if she were on the way to some sort of wild adventure. Part of that was finding out about Ozzie. This was a curiosity I had never seen. She didn't usually care to know people's stories. I sat in the front seat in amazement; who was this woman? She asked him what he did. He taught math. She liked that. She chatted: My mother was being charming. Friendly, even.

"And how do you know Alice?"

"I was good friends with Ronny a long time back."

"You mean the sheik of Araby?" she said.

I could see her grinning. "Yeah, Mom, the sheik."

And then she was off and running. "I hated him. He was weird."

"Can you stop?" I asked her.

"No, let me finish. And he had a brother. They both were weird."

"You know, Alice," Oz said, "I loved Ronny, but your mother's right, he was weird. Ethel, that's what we loved about him. What did we used to say? He was not like the other boys?"

Even that didn't turn her away from Ozzie. For a moment he was the prince on a horse, even if he was taking her to a dungeon, a high-rise in Queens.

"Let's call Andrew," I said. I dialed, he picked up. "Got Mom here, want to talk to her?"

She greedily grabbed the phone and rattled on as if the quicker she talked, the less she would have to feel.

After the cautious drive in darkness, Judi's neighborhood almost shocked, twinkling with an abundance of electricity. We pulled into the Bay Club. Oz stayed in the car, and I walked her into the building. In the elevator, Mom tugged on my sleeve and softly asked, "Is he married?"

I told her yes, he was. "Ah," she said, shook her head. I couldn't make out if it was with disappointment or approval. My cousin was waiting for her with hugs (there was nothing my mother hated more). "You're really leaving me here?" she whispered to me when I hugged her goodbye. The old Lido Hotel wasn't the only part of the picture moved off its mooring. So had Ethel.

## DRINK THIS

Milan Nestarec
Podfuck
Grape: Pinot Gris
Where: Moravia, Czech Republic

This has typical Nestarec electricity and plays tricks on me when I drink it. There's some oxidation on the nose—think a little orange juice in the sun, and a sludge brown color and I thought for sure the wine was going to taste like mud. Surprise! The taste was like the freshest peach juice, plump and dripping—the acidity makes it vibrant, and the skin contact gives it structure. Pinot gris? Really?

Years ago, at a friend's birthday party, I handed Frank Bruni—then the dining critic of the *New York Times*—a glass of something made from the pineau d'aunis grape from the Loire. He took a taste of a wine that I knew tasted just like Red Zinger tea, all rose-hippy, the (late) Christian Chaussard's Domaine le Briseau, Patapon. He burst out laughing. Isn't it the most beautiful response?

The night after wrenching my mother from her Long Beach, storm-battered cocoon, I could have used some of that delight as an antidote to the day. Because of the darkness, and the trouble navigating New York City during Sandy's immediate aftermath, I spent the night in Brooklyn with Ozzie and his wife and dog and cats. After looking over the wines Oz had stashed on his shelves, we settled on a pineau d'aunis. While I love them, they no longer surprise or shock me as they did the first time I tasted one. The one we drank was more serious than the Patapon. From Eric Nicolas, it was comforting, but looking back, if I were able to choose what I needed, it would have been a wine that made me laugh. One that shot me through with the shock of recognition. Something that could show life's absurdities even as it cozied up to tragedy. What I needed was a wine, any wine, from Milan Nestarec. The trouble is, in 2013 I didn't yet know he existed.

I first encountered Nestarec's wine a year later, at an importer's small trade tasting. There were about a hundred wines opened at their SoHo office, and I roamed around spitting, tasting, and taking notes. There were these unfamiliar bottles from the Czech Republic. I had been in Prague and had tasted some local wines back in 2004, so even though the area was more known for beer, I wasn't that surprised yet. Milan Nestarec 2013 stood staunchly on the table. It was from pinot gris (otherwise known as pinot grigio). Pinot gris (or grigio) is a white grape, but it has pink skins, so if you ferment it on the skins, you get a rosy color. Yet, Nestarec's wine wasn't pink or even reddish but brown and murky as muddy water. I was prepared for it to taste like death: spent, dry, ashen. The wine was called Podfuck. Save the shock, the word has a very different meaning in the Czech language, where it translates into something like "unexpected" or "cheat." Well, surprise! The wine tasted like fresh-pressed peaches. I needed to meet the wizard who'd made that thing.

Nestarec's village was in Moravia, just about an hour drive from Bratislava (in Slovakia), where I was staying on a book tour a few years after that initial taste. Heading to his place, I took in the land's rolling flatness, which felt a tad similar to the gentle bucolic landscape of Long Island's North Fork, with cornfields near the vines. Milan had made wine alongside his father since he was eleven; now in charge of the winery, he was taking it into a new and brave direction. He worked in a cramped and unromantic shed. But looks deceive.

With their monkey-like energy, Nestarec's wines did not disappoint. Turned out there was a growing clutch of others down there in the neighboring countries of the Czech Republic and Slovakia (in what I call the SloCzech region) who speak a similar wine language: fresh, original, shocking.

Despite the country's reputation for hops and being a princely region for beer drinking, the grapevine has been in Moravia ever since it arrived with the Romans. Wine was produced for centuries, until the Soviets put a kink in its commercial wine production, just as they did in all the USSR territories. Land was collectivized for the state, and volume was pushed way past the point where you could produce quality. The wine industry was converted to making bulk plonk. Old, indigenous vines were pulled out and new, productive European ones were put in.

The Communist government was out in 1989 with the Velvet Revolution, and winemaking began its slow revival. Four years later, Czechoslovakia split into two independent states. This "Velvet Divorce" birthed the Czech Republic and Slovakia. Slovakia lost 40 percent of its vineyards to Moravia. Today the grapes you find in neighboring Austria are the wines most prevalant in SloCzech, with riesling, müllerthurgau being top. There are also newer experimental grapes that actually aren't bad—like devín—thrown in. Here's the thing: The best of the wines from both sides have a breaking-the-boundary excitement, and yes, they're a little dangerous too. It was exactly what I would have prescribed for that night, a wine that got you out of a rut, moved foundations, showed life's absurdity, and made us laugh at our fragility but also reminded us of our resilience.


## DRINK THESE THOUGHT-PROVOKING WINES

I am entranced by what the post-Soviet countries are up to when it comes to wine. Here in the SloCzech, they are tapping into their inner artist. This is the avant-garde wine district: murky, funky, fizzy, and snappy. Expect more whites than reds, but the reds can be what a number of folks call crunchy—think more cranberry than plum; think fresh and alpine. The grapes are mostly familiar, like grüner veltliner, riesling (ryzlink rýnský), müller-thurgau, modrý Portugal (blauer portugieser), frankovka (blaufränkisch), and sure, your merlots and cabernets. Seek these people out and fasten your seat belts.

### Slo

Strekov 1075, Magula Family, Živé Víno, Slobodné Vinárstvo, Naboso

### Czech

Dlúhé Grefty, Jakub Novàk, Dobrá Vinice, Porta Bohemica, Richard Stavek, Milan Nestarec

### Extra Credit

Pineau d'aunis: If you love pinot noir and gamay, you owe it to yourself to experience pineau d'aunis. An older name for it is chenin noir, and its home territory is the Anjou and Touraine section of the Loire, where it often has the regional identifier of Coteaux du Loir. This charming grape fell out of favor in the seventies, because it was difficult to grow and the region wanted to simplify for consumers. Bad idea. A great loss. Scrounge around and see what you can find. The wines range from seriously beautiful to seriously lighthearted, in still and in sparkling.

Domaine de Bellivière, Béret et Compagnie, Bertin-Delatte, Domaine Deboutbertin, Domaine Les Grandes Vignes, Pascal Janvier, Les Maisons Rouge, Nana Vins et Cie, Domaine de la Roche Bleue, Brendan Tracey

# DATE WITH A SERIAL KILLER

The texts came in so fast they were like Morse code. Friends were sending me links to the news that Rodney Alcala, the Dating Game Serial Killer, was dead at seventy-seven. "How do you feel?" one asked.

Who knew? I had been grappling with that question for decades.

At the time of his death, Rodney Alcala had been convicted of only eight murders. He's suspected of scores of others throughout the United States and Europe. His preferred technique was a sordid mixture of rape, bondage, strangulation, mutilation. His killing string ended in 1980, when he was finally captured, landing on San Quentin's death row. But for most of my life, I thought of him as the pervert I escaped in 1969 when I was a depressed, bespectacled kid trapped in his East Village apartment. I told the story about getting away from the terrifying lunatic so many times, I nearly wore it out.

All of my bravado shrank on a night in 2010. I was in New Orleans on a work trip and turned on the news as I was packing to leave the next day. Instantly, I recognized the man on the screen in an Orange County courtroom. Beady eyes behind glasses. Greasy, wavy hair. Pointed Adam's apple. Words scrolled at the bottom of the screen: "Rodney Alcala, Sentenced to Death."

"No," I blurted out loud even though I was the only one in the room. "He's Jon Berger."

169

I had never heard of the Dating Game Serial Killer or Alcala, but he was definitely the very same photographer, Jon, who had accosted me in a bookstore on St. Marks Place in 1969, Roman Polanski's student at NYU. That cockeyed face was the same, if decades older. I'd spent one very long hour with him so long ago that it didn't seem possible I could remember what he looked like.

Hoping for once that my mother was right, that I had an overactive imagination, I Googled the killer through the night. After a few hours of grisly details that I couldn't look away from, I came across one of his aliases: John (or Jon) Burger (or Berger). The man had arrived in the East Village in late 1968, a photographer enrolled at New York University. Denial was no longer an option, and I was overwhelmed with self-flagellation: How could I have been so fatally dumb? And how could I have been so lucky.

As dawn crept in and I read all that the Internet had to offer back in 2010, I read how he, a cocky, handsome guy with a square jaw, got his nickname from being the winning bachelor on a 1978 episode of *The Dating Game*. His date found him creepy and refused the "dream" date. That rejection might have kicked off a killing spree that ended with the heartbreaking murder of twelve-year-old Robin Samsoe and his last moments as a free man. By the time I boarded the flight back home, I was shaking, as if someone had pulled me back from an oncoming car. Instead of feeling thankful, I kept perseverating on the question—how had I been allowed to live.

Once home, I still couldn't let go of the destruction I had sidestepped that day in 1969. Alcala had pleaded with me to let him photograph me, and as it turned out, his favored hunting method involved his camera. A locker full of photographs from the sixties and seventies, discovered in Seattle, was posted online with a general call to the public for help identifying the subjects. Those photos kept on calling me, and I spent weeks looking through the sometimes self-conscious, eerily innocent and beautiful images, looking for my young self with my frizzed-out red hair. I wasn't among them. When the news hit the *Times* that Alcala was being extradited to New York to sit trial for the murders of Cornelia Crilley and Ellen Hover, I knew I'd be there.

Reading the news, I noticed the name of the cold-case detective, Wendell Stradford, who had played Ahab to Alcala's Moby. I reached out to him on Facebook, of all places, referring to myself as "one who got away."

Stradford was kind and we talked frequently. He encouraged me to go to the trial. Perhaps I'd get some sort of closure, he suggested. I stammered that I didn't need closure. After all, I was alive, I hadn't been harmed. I merely was saddled with survivor's guilt. "Go," he said.

In December 2012 I took my place in the 100 Centre Street courtroom, as family members of the dead lectured Alcala on his lack of remorse and humanity. I bowed my head under their pain. I felt finished with it all. But by March I felt compelled to visit Alcala while he was in Rikers waiting his return to California. "I can't understand my impulse," I said to the detective.

"Trust your instinct," Stradford told me. "Who knows, he might open up to you and lead us to more bodies. And if you end up writing a book or something, you'll be giving voice to those who can't speak." He armed me with a sense of greater purpose than my need to stare down my past.

Stradford provided me with reams of faded army-discharge reports, court transcripts, and FBI files. They sat on my desk in a red plastic folder for a few weeks as I gathered up the courage to look at them. I was the kid who'd always avoided horror films. Serial killers? Not interested, had never seen or read *The Silence of the Lambs*. I wasn't going to write a book and live with the Alcala horror for years. Finally, I picked up the folder and sat on my couch.

An eight-year-old Alcala painted his scrotum and penis with his brother's airplane paints. The drying paint hurt him, and so he reached for the paint remover, which proved excruciating. When he went AWOL from the army in 1963, he committed what seemed to be his first registered serious crime, a car and credit card theft, an assault on a man and another on a woman. He landed in jail and then the army psychiatric ward. He was soon court-martialed and discharged honorably. Five years later, months before my encounter with him, he brutalized an eight-year-old named Tali in Los Angeles. A witness saw a struggle as Alcala dragged her into an abandoned house where he raped her, beat her, and finally pressed a metal pipe over her throat. When cops knocked on the front door, he disappeared out the rear one. I read of the gristle, bone, and blood of his victims' deaths. Stradford said that there were two other New Yorkers he knew of who had escaped Alcala. One of them, Lisa, had encountered him in 1978. She was only seventeen and had just landed on the West Coast to find a new adventurous life. "Call her?" he asked me. "I think she needs to talk."

I left a message and carefully dropped Wendell's name like a calling card. Lisa called me back. She soon told me her story, her voice trembling.

"I was new in San Francisco and so excited to be free. It was the night that the Grateful Dead were closing Winterland," she told me. "At an after-party, I met Alcala there. He invited me to go with him to Half Moon Bay, where he said his friends had horses we could ride on the beach as long as we groomed them." He was handsome. She assumed he was safe. She agreed.

They hitchhiked in the dark night, and when she saw a deserted property off Highway 1 and no stables, she knew she was in trouble. He dragged her to a barn. Chickens were running everywhere. "He shoved a huge piece of furniture against the door and pushed me up a ladder. There was a round bed. All around, I saw items that belonged to girls. Pocketbooks, clothing, identification. Truly bad things happened there. I started beating myself up for being so naive. He ripped my pants so hard they tore into pieces. I played like I was into it, I didn't know what else to do. I didn't want to be killed. I knew not to fight back; when in trouble, stay calm." She laughed uncomfortably. As she took a breath, I relived the mess in the Sixth Street apartment, the women's artifacts, the ghostly bone truth I felt, terrible things happened there.

In the morning, he seemed totally different, calm. He shoved the heavy piece of furniture he had blocked the door with and let her leave—bloody, beaten, her clothes in rags. "He said to me, 'I owe you a pair of jeans,' and I said, 'That's okay.'" It was still hard for Lisa to forgive herself for being young and naive. I understood. We had a bond, even though we wore different scars.

Unlike my subsequent visit to San Quentin, all I had needed to get into Rikers was identification, Alcala's prisoner number, and a submissive attitude. The staff were nasty and abusive, and after a very rude strip search, I waited in a holding room where the cheerful Dolly Parton was promoting a new book on the blaring television. I nervously paced in front of the TV, suddenly seized by stage fright. What was I doing there? How was I even going to start the conversation? I finally decided to go with "You see we met a long time ago."

The time came. I walked to meet him. He approached me, unshackled; I wasn't expecting that. He grinned at me as if I were a long-lost girlfriend. I wanted to turn and run but sucked in my breath and sat down on the orange Formica chair in what looked like a schoolroom. Alcala did not remember me, but he said he'd try to the next time. What chutzpah, I thought. Another time?

"Yes, go," Stradford said to me. "Maybe you'll write a book, maybe not, but as he wants to see you again, you have a rapport with him, maybe he'll give you some clues to others he might have killed."

Perhaps, I told myself, this was a way I could give meaning to why I'd survived. Help those still looking for their missing daughters, sisters, wives, giving others closure. I was willing to go.

In order to visit a prisoner in San Quentin, I had to first request permission in writing from Alcala. But how was I to address a serial killer? "Dear"? "Mr. Alcala"? Having to play the line between my repulsion and seduction, I went with "Mr. Alcala." His reply was more personal.

*Dear Alice!!!!!*

*I simply cannot believe that you have just been approved to visit me!!!!!*

*So whenever you want to come down, come on down. I'm looking forward to your visit! What more can I say? Well, I can say that you're the first non-family person other than legal, investigators, etc., that has been approved to visit me!!! Boy, are you lucky!*

*Sincerely,*
*Rodney*

If that was the extent of my luck in life, I was in very deep trouble. A few letters later, he wrote to tell me how much he was looking forward to my visit and signed it "Love, Rodney." I had to muscle myself through thoughts that my visit was fodder for his sexual fantasies.

In my previsit phone call, a Sergeant Meredith had given me the dress code: no cleavage (as if), no hanging earrings, no colors associated with prisoners or guards—blue, green, orange, and yellow were out. No underwire bras, which was a problem, since those were all I had. I could bring photographs and a bag of quarters. "For what?" I asked. The answer was "For the treats."

Befuddled, I called Stradford. "I'm supposed to feed him?"

"Think of the zoo," Stradford said. "Feed him, and he'll cooperate."

I called Lisa on the way to the airport and told her I was flying west to San Quentin. "My God," she said, "you're so brave."

She had been the brave one. Not me, not by a long shot.

"Listen," she said in a voice so sweet, "could you see if he remembers me?"

She and I had the same need for acknowledgment. To understand that we had not imagined what had happened to us; that it was real and so was our survival.

I flew out to California and a good friend dropped me off at the barbed-wire end of a sleepy cul-de-sac. I said good-bye and got out of his car in my new prison-approved attire, clutching the Ziploc of quarters. "You're crazy for going," he said. And promised to come back to fetch me. I was allowed a whole eight hours, but I figured three were good enough.

Stowing my belongings in a locker, I went through security, gripping my driver's license, the Ziploc of change. I asked the officer where I needed to go and she pointed to the faux Windsor Castle, complete with Gothic windows and jagged crenellations up a hill. "You're going to the squat one to its right," she instructed.

In my Riker's visit Alcala had cursed that jail's plagues: the weather, the food, and its lack of aesthetic. In comparison, San Quentin's death row was deluxe. Those views of the glassine bay? Priceless. Walking uphill, I passed an ancient well that looked quaint enough until I was hit with the stench of dead fish collected at its bottom. Disgusted, I ran to my destination and walked up the short flight of steps.

The room had a series of free-standing visiting pens. It was noisy and mammoth, like some football field–size kennel. The officer demanded my identification and placed it in a book. "Will I get that back?" I asked, trying for comic relief. No answer. "Vending machines?" I asked.

He waved to the rear. "Get what you need, and we'll get your prisoner."

With my stash of quarters, I stood in front of the oracle of vending machines and wondered which piece of crap behind the plastic would be the truth serum. At Rikers, Alcala had bragged about his love of fitness and his disdain for fat, so I scanned past the Doritos and Pringles for something that could pass as nutritious. The plastic-wrapped orange was shriveled. The apple looked mealy. So what if I got the murderer the wrong snack? Pissed off at myself for caring, I hastily grabbed a yogurt and trail mix and went to the front of the line to wait.

Most people had gotten there early to make the most of their time. There was a thrum of activity: talking, playing checkers, doing puzzles, reading newspapers, whispering close to each other, grasping for intimacy.

A guard escorted me through the room. Alcala approached, handcuffed from behind. As I walked down our row, I saw Alcala enter the cage and turn his back to the guard, who unlocked his hands through the metal chicken wire. The visiting space was about a third the size of my railroad apartment's bedroom but big enough for two folding chairs, a card table, and some deep breaths. Only after Alcala was seated, his arms and legs free, did the guard let me in. I took the other chair. At seventy-one, his skin resembled a parched, stretched canvas; his tightly waved long hair was parted in the middle, just as I remembered it, only now it was silvery. He had an aged-hippie look. I could smell his nasty prison soap, caustic like Ajax.

In that jangly cell, his face had a deerlike stillness. I tried not to be obvious when I stole a glance downward. He wore canvas loafers secured to his feet with fabric straps. The FBI files explained in detail how he strangled his victims with shoestrings or panty hose. He might have looked frail, but I knew that if the adrenaline coursed through his veins, he could twist my neck before any guard could reach us. Worried that fear might excite him, I sat on my hands, which were trembling despite an outward bravado.

He smiled. As in photos I'd seen of another serial killer, Ted Bundy, there were some angles where he looked deranged and others, handsome.

As I laid the snacks out on the table, I told him, "I know you like healthy things. I didn't have many options."

He glanced at my offerings, then, like a little boy who got vanilla instead of chocolate, said, "I like oranges."

"The orange was moldy," I said.

"Next time," he said.

He seemed to have no recollection of my Rikers visit. This stunned me, as the man who boasted he was a member of Mensa couldn't remember one of the few visitors he'd had since 1980. I wondered whether he had some dementia or perhaps he was playing me. We sat for too many beats without conversation. I couldn't tolerate the silence, so I opened with pretty much the same script as in Rikers. "We met many years ago."

He nodded politely. "Where?"

"In New York City."

"I loved New York," he said, his face living the memory.

Of course he did, he was on the lam from his ghastly assault on an eight-year-old Tali Shapiro and had hopped a flight to New York to be swallowed up into the anonymity of the city, hunting for victims.

"What year did we meet in?" he asked.

"Nineteen sixty-nine," I said. "I was curious if you remembered me."

"That was a long time ago," he said.

"Yes, but my situation was a little unusual."

I told him how he'd followed me out of a bookstore and persisted until I agreed to model for him on his rooftop, around the corner from the Fillmore East. He'd known I was a dancer, and he'd asked me to leap and twirl while he photographed, talking about his unhappy childhood. We'd both had fathers who screwed around.

"It started to thunder and rain. I helped you carry your equipment to your apartment," I said.

"You waved a kimono in my direction and told me to slip into it. That's when I said I had to go."

He seemed to be enjoying this tale of mine. I continued, "You asked me to wait a bit. You wanted me to see something. You handed me a stack of Polaroids. You wanted to know what I thought. Then you went into the bathroom."

The memory of those pictures flashed in front of me, though I didn't tell him. A naked woman lying on her side. Another on her knees. The third, a teenager. My age? All of them still or doll-like.

As if it were his prison bedtime story, Alcala shifted to his chair's edge, waiting for me to go on.

"I was at the door when you came out of the bathroom. Just before you could reach me, I ran out." I had no idea how I'd managed that lock.

I went on, "Here's the thing, though: I left my book on your cabinet, right near the door. I went back to get it. That's the part I thought you'd recall."

"What is so unusual about going back for what you left?" he asked.

I did not want to titillate, so while trying to be as clinical as could be, I reiterated, You were naked from the waist down with an erection. You were about to rape me, possibly kill me, and yet I returned. I pounded on your door and shouted, "My book, please!"

What a monumental act of stupidity. I still wonder what my returning in outrage said about who I was and who I became. Like Lisa, could I forgive myself my embarrassing naïveté?

"You opened the door, pants back on, but not zipped."

I remembered deftly snatching the paperback from him. "As I ran down the stairs, you pleaded, 'Just let me mastur-bate.'"

A flutter of concern flashed in his eyes and Alcala softly asked me, "Did I hurt you?"

I answered him, "You did me no physical harm."

He seemed relieved. But I wondered, was that where my oft-crippling social anxiety came from? Was that when this fog of fear that I clawed through all my life was born? Was that where it started?

"I have another story for you," I said, and told him an ab-breviated version of Lisa's story, parts he might remember. The house on Half Moon Bay. The promise of horses. "In the morning, you said you were sorry and told her, 'I owe you a pair of pants,' because you had ripped them to shreds." I looked at him. His eyes barely moved, but I could almost smell his ten-sions, as if I was going to fly into an accusation. "Familiar?"

"No," Alcala told me.

I would have thought he would remember those he let live, since there were so many more he did not.

"You know I didn't kill all of the people they said I did," he added.

"Of course you did," I said.

He looked past me and then sighed, almost convincingly. "I can't remember any of it. But I regret it all."

"How can you regret what you can't remember?" I asked, feeling his lying.

"I only remember the good things," he said. "If Lisa can tell me something good about that night, maybe that would help."

*Like not killing her?* I wanted to ask. What better outcome could there be?

"You didn't kill her. I think I know why," I said, understanding that Lisa had not resisted, had let him delude himself it was a date, and therefore had not inflamed his anger with rejection. "But why didn't you kill me?" I asked.

"I didn't hurt the people I took photographs of. I have a big scrapbook of all my girlfriends' photographs. I'll show you."

I realized he was confusing the locker of photographs with his fantasy scrapbook. I wasn't buying it and pushed back. "Of course you killed some of them."

His lip twitched.

"Do you want me to give you their names?" I countered fast, without even registering that I was getting a serial killer very angry. "You were out with your camera when you took Robin."

His fist clenched; his face seemed even more lopsided. I saw that mentioning her name enraged him. He could strangle me before a guard could get to me. Hothead, I chastised myself. I reversed tone and quietly asked, "Do you ever think about getting out?"

The tactic worked, and he answered, "At least here, I'm not hurting anyone."

Was it an actual confession that he gave me? I wondered for a second and then dismissed his answer. Not genuine. But in the calm that followed, he stunned me by being curious. "What do you do?" he asked me.

I decided to tell the truth. "I'm a wine writer."

"Really?" His flat affect perked right up. He clapped his

hands together in delight as he said, "I love wine," using the present tense. "What do you like to drink? What are your favorites?"

One of the more notorious serial killers in the States was hitting me up for wine recommendations like some guy I might meet at a party. I almost laughed at the absurdity. Really, like I was going to talk about the wines from clay jars in Georgia or the Loire's diversity? Or ask him what he enjoyed drinking? But then I flashed to 1969. Walking down Second Avenue when he'd let me believe he was a fellow Jew. He'd claimed he too loved the baked apples at Rapoport's, the dairy restaurant next to the Fillmore. Decades later, he was using those same moves, feigning commonalities, right there on death row. As in the story of the scorpion and the frog, psychopathy was his nature. I motioned for the guard to get me out of there.

I ran down the hill, past that putrid fish smell. I reclaimed my bag from the locker and then sat on the curb, on the freedom side of the barbed wire, with my notepad and pen, while I waited for my friend to drive up. I tried to get it all down, to record every detail of what had happened, what was said, before I blinked it all away.

Had I crossed the country expecting Alcala to say, "Yes. That girl. The one I promised a new pair of pants to? Lisa? Tell her yes. I remember." Or that he would tell me where he'd killed the others? It's rather an absurd notion, going to a serial killer for resolution, to find out why he didn't kill me. Instead, I'd found a killer who was playing mind games up until the end. I had to deal with my survival and their deaths on my own.

## DRINK THIS

Martin Ray
Pinot Noir
Saratoga, California, USA

The color of the wine, over a half century old, was like tomato water. The taste ping-ponged from bright to leather to
Band-Aid to delicate to intense to gorgeous, to alive to electric
and mushroom power and back to Burgundy and then to the
moon and then to the umami of Japan and the acid was out
of control.

José, my Spanish wine importer friend, was just a few minutes late. Seeing him down the road, I shoved my pen and notebook back into my bag, pulled myself up from the curb, and ran to the car.

"Sorry, sorry," he said, as if he had made me wait in hell.

"I'm okay," I said.

"You're loca, Mrs. Feiring."

"Loca or not, get us out of here," I told him. In a flash we were onto 101 as if speeding away from a disaster.

"Well?" he asked me.

Staring out the window, I wasn't yet ready to talk about my experience. "He asked me which wines I liked to drink. Can you believe that?"

"That's insane," José said to me.

What was the correct activity after visiting a convicted serial killer of animalistic crimes? I could have jumped into the Pacific to purge. Run a marathon to outpace the spirits. Sweated it out in hot springs. Dropped acid and gone even deeper. But as the proper methodology is not listed in any of the rule books, I headed to the vineyard. José and I had been eager to see the historic Martin Ray vines above Santa Cruz, the ones that Duncan Arnot and Nathan Roberts made an impressive pinot from. We made a call and we were soon following the winemakers south on 101.

Martin Ray was a visionary and an essential piece of American wine history. Similar to many of the passionate and opinionated, Ray was generally viewed as a difficult nutcase and in the 1960s when he proudly stated that he neither added to nor took away from his wines, it was wildly ahead of its time. After all, that is the mantra of today's natural wine movement.

An hour and a half later, we were on corkscrew roads climbing Mount Eden, fourteen hundred feet up, new developments and sprawling houses punctuating the wilderness. The late Ray would have been pissed.

The vineyard gate was a wooden corral sort of thing. Nathan, the bicyclist-slender winemaker, in a baseball cap, opened the road up for us. He and his high school friend Duncan were among the first of the new crop of Californians seeking to strip the new American wine to its core, lower alcohol, less fruit-forward, and more soul. They had exposed a part of California I had rarely seen, and I liked it. In addition, they were obsessed with Ray as well.

Born in 1904, Ray often spent time in vineyards of his neighbor, Paul Masson. Masson, another essential man in modern wine history, was French, from Burgundy, and had brought pinot noir cuttings from his home region to the mountaintop, where he mentored and befriended little Martin. Martin grew up to be a stockbroker, which might have been the right fit for his parents but never was for him; he suffered a nervous breakdown in the 1930s, and after that, he took a turn back to the vines. He was convinced that California could be world-class and pushed it. In the 1940s, when everyone else was making jug or sweet wine, he grew cabernet, chardonnay, and pinot. When everyone else was making blends, he bottled his wines as 100 percent varietals.

Ray railed against additive addition (we had that in common). He also lobbied hard for appellation designation. If you can go into a store and order a cabernet, you probably have Mr. Ray to thank. It is because of him that we think of California in terms of regions—that Napa is different from Sonoma and different from Paso Robles.

They took us into the vineyard, where the soils were baking in the sun. "So how was the serial killer?" Duncan asked.

"Surreal," I said, and was grateful he let it alone. I wanted to wash off the spirits and turn the page.

Ray's efforts were controversial and reportedly ranged from the ridiculous to the sublime. He refused to add the stabilizing antibacterial sulfur dioxide, which led to the unpredictable nature of his wine. Some said one out of ten was drinkable, and I longed to drink one, to see something of the past, what he was like. I had given up hope that a kindly collector would make that possible.

I stood with my hands on my hips, the wind blowing, and looked down the mountain to the next hilltop and the scalloped vineyards of another winery. The air was full of the aromas of the flowering vines. The perfume was like Dove soap, but in a good way.

The dry-farmed grapevines stood up individually, like soldiers. Dwarfing me. Each had been tied to a single stake, pole-bean-style, like the Northern Rhône *échalas* but with a floppy, top-heavy California sprawl to keep the grapes shaded from the intense sun. The soil was broken reddish soil, Franciscan shale. Duncan told us, "Martin Ray referred to that as "rotten rock." I could almost feel Martin, whose ashes had been scattered in those soils in 1976. The air was very clean and warm on my skin. I reveled in it.

"Let's eat!" Nathan declared after we had walked over the land, through Martin's house packed with mementos, and through the small garage where Martin had made his wine. I wasn't hungry, yet the two had lugged a red and white cooler with them down from Sonoma, so we retreated to a table and unloaded the tabbouleh and the sausage for the meat eaters. The wineglasses set out meant there was something coming.

Nathan pulled out a bottle of Martin Ray. "We pick them up at auction when we can," Nathan said as José grabbed it to look at the label. I let out a whoop. A wine dream come true. It was a 1962 pinot from that very vineyard.

"I can't believe this," I said, looking at the generosity in front of me, eyes welling up with tears. It wasn't just a bottle; it was connection. In 1962 Alcala's estranged father had died. The whole family attended the funeral, and shortly after, the violence began, but in 1962, Alcala's victims were still safe. There it was, Alcala, Alcala, Alcala. Why not me. Martin Ray, I would imagine, would have no patience for my survivor's guilt. I pulled myself together. I turned to the wine.

The color of the wine was oxidized-blood brown. We all sank our noses in to catch what it had to tell us. It was a crapshoot, one in ten, so they said. The smell ignited. We all could tell that before we even tasted. "This is legit!" Duncan yelled. The wine was alive.

José, who loves his old wine, just kept on shaking his head in awe. I took another sip. I wasn't spitting even if it was the afternoon, because I was being forced to confront life.

Ray's name was sold, and today, the Martin Ray winery of Sonoma has absolutely no heritage or aesthetic connection to its namesake. To taste the wines made from the Peter Martin Ray vineyard, head for the wineries to whom Martin's stepson sells fruit. Duncan and Nathan get all of the pinot noir, and if you're fortunate enough to get one of the bottles that don't have any added sulfur dioxide, you'll be lucky indeed.

## DRINK THESE MARTIN RAY VINEYARDS WINES

Ceritas (cabernet and chardonnay)
Birichino (cabernet)
Jaimee Motley (cabernet)
Arnot-Roberts (pinot noir)

# Tale of Two Stones

My father had been dead for six years, still didn't have a tombstone, and his older sister, Ruth, was getting impatient. On a winter's night, while she shouted at me through the phone, I imagined her finger jabbing the air as she threatened me, "We will do it ourselves and we'll never tell you. Take your hatred of your father to the grave!"

But our aunt was wrong about our delay with Dad's stone. We weren't motivated by the hatred she thought we had for him. We simply had writers' block.

Dad was much loved by his siblings. To his nieces and nephews, Uncle Phil was a legend. He was the relative you could talk to about anything. He'd pay for your abortion, he'd get you off the hook if busted for pot. He was the only one allowed to visit the hospital after a suicide attempt. Uncle Phil was a category all his own.

However, Andrew and I had a different narrative. Not much of a role model. So when it came time to put up the stone—which, according to Jewish custom, happens within a year of death—we stalled.

Only in hindsight do I see the callousness of our fribbling. I should have been sympathetic; after all, Aunt Ruth loved her younger brother just as I did my older. My first word was not Mommy or Daddy, it was Andrew. My first memory was Andrew picking me up out of my crib. We finger-picked our guitars together, singing out "I Ain't Marchin' Anymore" until we were hoarse. We dug through our father's underwear drawer seeking the clues for whom Dad was cheating with and when he would leave home. When I, a depressed teen, hitched in an attempted runaway, my destination—though I didn't make it—was directly to Andrew's dorm room. The one person I entrusted with my near-death experience in 1969? That's right.

It went both ways: In trouble, he contacted me, even if the method was unconventional, like the time he was in medical school in Manila, thousands and thousands of miles away, and I was at our mother's for summer break. On a June night in the mid-seventies, I drifted to sleep, when his voice woke me up. "I'm scared shitless," I heard him say. I snapped awake and thought, It was a dream. I drifted off again, and it happened again. With the same words. I could feel his fear. This was not a mistake.

I stumbled sleepily into my mother's bedroom. "Mom. Mom, we must call Andrew. He's in trouble."

"You're going insane," she said. "Go to sleep."

She always feared my sensitivity, worried that it was a sign that maybe I'd go nuts like my grandfather's sister did. My father had told me Tante Feige used to cackle like a chicken, and when she was about fifty, she was found naked on a bench in Brooklyn in a snowstorm and died a few days later in Brookdale Hospital.

I went back to bed. Andrew wouldn't let me sleep. I stormed into my mother's bedroom and insisted. I was having none of this "you're crazy" business. My brother needed us. I grabbed my phone book and looked up his number. It took a few tries but I finally reached the Philippines. Andrew's roommate answered and told us he was in the hospital. It turned out he had a severe and mysterious inflammation in an indiscreet place. He would be fine, but he was terrified: His future sex life and children were in peril. When he came home, he brought me a little present—a wood carving of a man in a wine barrel. When you slid the cask off, the guy's wooden penis went *boing*! My brother had attached a note, a little piece of Andrew's wisdom.

Andrew went on to marry his college sweetheart, move to Milwaukee, and have a family. Our lives couldn't be more different. Through it all, he remained not only my brother but my best friend and the father Philip should have been.

Ever since Dad died in 2004, we had feverishly fixated and bonded over our task. But we could not solve the puzzle of the proper wording. How could we be truthful about our feelings yet memorialize the love he inspired? We weren't being flippant; for us, the responsibility of the stone was too heavy.

Even our mother got into the act, suggesting "My Way," the tune Dad whistled as he left her in 1972. Andrew and I thought we might give his siblings and their children top billing, "Beloved Brother and Uncle Phil," omitting ourselves. Perhaps that would work. The stone had long since been paid for, and we were late and running out of ideas and excuses.

As his kids grew older, Andrew took to visiting several times a year solo. It really did feel like he was a bigamist sneaking off to see his other family, his sister and mother. His pattern was to arrive Sunday morning and leave Monday evening. We had a ritual. Ethel would pick me up, then we'd pick him up, and then we'd play. One frigid Sunday afternoon, we spent hours in the Second Avenue movie theater; too cold to leave, we stayed for the second feature, the first Borat film, and couldn't quite believe that Ethel doubled over with laughter. There were museums. Every other year we'd hit the long-dead relatives. At night we'd both sleep over with her in Long Beach. Monday morning we all piled into the car; Ethel went to work at the jewelry exchange that was a ten-minute walk from my apartment. Andrew and I would then spend the day hanging out, mostly parallel working with talk breaks until Mom took him to his Midwest Express flight back home. Sometime in between visits, Andrew said, "Have you heard from Ruth?"

"No, now that you bring it up," I said.

"*Hmmm*," he said.

"Right," I said. "Next time you're in, let's take a ride?"

It was a clammy August Sunday in 2011 when my mother, who should have been a taxi driver instead of the most senior jeweler left on the Bowery, drove from Long Beach to fetch me from New York City. After that, we picked up Andrew from LaGuardia. Then we headed out east to Mount Ararat Cemetery to see if Aunt Ruth had made good on her threat. On the way, the catch-up was the usual: my next travels to vines, Andrew's latest invention for angioplasty techniques, Mom's complaining about the cost of a carat stone.

"It's a maze here," Andrew observed as Mom navigated through Mount Ararat to find my father's family plot. We slammed car doors and let our nimble not-quite-ninety-year-old mother blaze the way, swinging her Pepto-Bismol-pink pocketbook.

Sure enough, next to our paternal grandparents was a rock flush with the crabgrass bearing the name Philip T. Feiring.

"Do you want to know what the T stood for?" Mom asked even though we'd heard the story over and over again. "When he went to law school, he thought he needed a middle name. So he took the T for *tuchas*."

Andrew and I stood side by side, looked down, and saw "Beloved Brother, Uncle, Father, Grandfather." Aunt Ruth did it her way.

I waited for my brother's reaction, observing him. Fancy cardiologist or not, he still dressed as he had in college: faded jeans, button-down shirt, pocket jammed with pens; all he was missing was his ponytail. All Andrew's face revealed was a pensive lower lip, as if to say, "Well, there you go."

Honestly, we were more relieved than disturbed, and we packed into the air-conditioned car and headed to Cedarhurst for kosher sushi. Andrew looked pale, a little green. "You okay?" I asked as he popped a couple of TUMS.

"I've been having this thing," he said, tapping his chest, "but I'm okay."

As usual, on the day of his flight, we spent hours together. He worked on an angioplasty PowerPoint. I got ready for yet another book research trip to the country of Georgia. We took breaks. We'd walk through the Lower East Side where he picked up a chocolate babka for his wife. We laughed. We rehashed the past. Late in the afternoon, he wanted a cup of coffee. I ground the beans. I brewed. He took more TUMS. I said to him, "Hey Doc, I know you never go to doctors but maybe you should?"

"I'm fine," he said again.

The next day he called me and asked, "Did you find anything on the kitchen table?"

"No," I said. "Did you leave something behind?"

"Call me if you do." He was cryptic.

I went on a treasure hunt. There on the table was his unwashed coffee cup. When I'm in a writing zone, these details often escape me. "I am the worst housekeeper!" I admonished myself. Humiliated, I picked it up and, like a salamander under a rock, something was hiding. A folded check. It scared me at first, like some terrible omen. I had never asked him for money, nor had he ever given me any. Then, all of those years when I worried that perhaps he shared my mother's disapproval for my life vanished. That check was unprecedented and for me, five hundred dollars was sizable. I went off to Georgia not penny-pinching as much as I would have otherwise. I tormented myself when we found out his prognosis; why hadn't I intuited his illness? He must have known then. Why else would he have been so sentimental?

After his diagnosis my mother and I flew to Milwaukee as often as we could. I brought cashmere caps to keep Andrew's head warm and wines to show him why the world of wine had captivated me. We sat at his dining room table, the bottle of Heinz as a centerpiece. I opened a Georgian wine. "Remember the woman who kept silkworms who wanted you to come to Georgia so she could heal you?" I asked. "This isn't hers. Lamara only makes her wine for home consumption. But this one is made from close by her place." The wine was the color of rattlesnake venom. I had no idea how it would match with the chemotherapy he was taking. "Nice," he said. Drinking that wine was the closest I was going to get to sharing life with him, a last attempt.

He and I talked or texted daily, struggling to snuggle into the closeness we had assumed we would have time for in old age. A little after a full year of treatment, my sister-in-law told us to come the next day. Stay the night, then leave. She was in charge, after all.

We had less than twenty-four hours to spend with him. When we arrived in Milwaukee, I walked up to his bedroom, and saw him in his blue scrubs, clutching his pillow, in a morphine haze. I felt I could read into his restlessness, wanting it to be over and wanting to cling to his life all at once.

The next day I barely left his room. When he was sleeping, I looked around. There was his Valentine's Day letter to his wife. The picture of their long-ago trip—two kids in love in a black-eyed Susan field in Scotland. My mother was timid, not knowing what to do. Seeing him tangled up in the blankets, she paced and parsed, "This is not happening. I believe in miracles. This is not happening."

From under the covers, Andrew said with as much might as he could muster, "Not helpful, Mom."

She left the room and went to the kitchen to visit with her grandchildren. Time was running out. In an hour, I led her up the stairs.

"Go in and say goodbye," I ordered her. "And tell him you love him."

"He knows I love him," she said, showing her superpower, denial.

For a moment, I was unable to talk. I knew how hard it was for her but living without having had that final moment would be so much worse and so I pushed back at her firmly. "This is the last time you will ever be able to tell him. So, go."

I stood by the door, listening, grateful when she got the words out.

Seven days later, we were back to take him to his new home. It was a rainy, stormy, muddy day. He was sixty-two.

On the year anniversary of his death, we would normally gather graveside to take a ceremonial gauze cloth off a stone

195

and then eat the traditional bagel and lox. I was dreading the call to let us know the date for his unveiling and book our flights. I feared going back to the cemetery; I wasn't ready. None of us were. Instead, on his *yahrzeit,* my sister-in-law sent me some digitals of the monument. In poignant contrast to the way Andrew and I had handled our father's headstone, his had gone up swiftly. The words carved in the granite were unapologetic and erasing: "Andrew Jonathan Feiring, beloved husband and father."

It sliced me in a way I couldn't have imagined. There was no Jewish law requiring the mention of a sister or a surviving mother. There was no law at all, it was merely custom. But like most traditions around death, they were in place more for the living. Andrew would have laughed and tried to soothe me. "Why do you need that affirmation?" he would have said. "Mouse, it doesn't matter. Really. It doesn't."

My brother left notes, and not only under coffee cups. Like a silly girl looking for a sign from the dead, my eyes floated up above my desk to the books of wine research and Philip Roth. Right next to *Sabbath's Theater* was that local-craft tchotchke Andrew had sent me long ago. I always placed the wooden man like a totem close to my work spaces, from Selectric to Macintosh. Having not removed the barrel from the toy man in years, I slipped it off. All hinged appendages went *boing.* I saw that the small piece of paper was still taped to its torso, a note that my brother had written, the content I had long since forgotten. But there in faded indigo ink was: "Alice, hang in there, Love Andy."

## DRINK THIS

Marina Mtsvane
Grape: Mtsvane
Where: Kartli, Georgia

Marina Kurtanidze, the first woman winemaker in Georgia, got these grapes from Manavi, where the best mtsvane grapes are said to come from. She ferments everything—skins, pips, and stalks—in those buried clay pots called *qvevri*, for five months. The modestly amber-colored wine is singing. Preserved lemon with its salted rind, textural for sure, and thirst quenching.

We parked the car outside a tall cement wall. Lamara Bezhashvili lived behind it with her mother, sheep, goats, rabbits, chickens, a spooky blue-eyed cat, snake-eating birds, mulberry trees, and silkworms.

Near fifty at the time, Lamara could have been sent from central casting to play a fairy-tale raven-haired beauty. But more to the point, she had a vivacious spirit and magnetic energy and somehow managed to remain single in a culture where having a family was essential. Yet she had other children: silkworms. Lamara was one of the last of the silk-growing and -spinning artisans in Georgia.

Entering the worm shacks, I had the feeling I was in a recently vacated summer camp bunkhouse. There were the insects that had not just vacated but died for our pleasure, their silk already stuffed in bags, ready to be spun.

This was the second time I had come to Georgia to launch one of my books that had been translated into their curly language. Uneasy about my brother, I had agreed to go, with the caveat that it had to be a quick trip. As jam-packed as my schedule was, my American-expat winemaking friend John had insisted on taking me to see a close friend of his. He hadn't told me why.

Lamara had assumed I wanted to see how she worked, and she demonstrated, turning her nimble thumb and fore-finger into a spindle. There was a slight chill in the air and she stood with her fingers wrapped in silky filaments when John told her, "Alice's brother is very sick."

She flinched, and I felt embarrassed to be sharing this with a stranger, no matter how lovely.

"What kind?" she asked, knitting her dark eyebrows to-gether.

"Pancreatic," I said.

She shook her head. "Stage?"

"Four," I said. "Is there any other kind?"

I saw what John had been thinking. He was trying to help in the way he knew how. Lamara, as it turned out, wasn't just the last hand-silk spinner on the Silk Route; she was also the keeper of ancient medical remedies. In the way that people can't resist asking me for wine advice, people couldn't stop asking Lamara for the cures, and she couldn't stop offering them. She put her craft down and said to me very solemnly, "Send him to me. I'll heal him."

Looking around at the animals, the rusticity, the outhouse, I knew there was no way my brother, a Western medical man, would have given her powers a shot. I promised I would try to convince him. Is there anything stronger than a deadly cancer to make a skeptic grasp for something supernatural? I yearned to accept the fantasy that she would cure him with her little bag containing specks of translucent rocks, for which she could not find the English name. It turned out it was alum, three times a day stuck under his tongue, then take three days off. Repeat the cycle for ten days. Also one glass of yarrow tea three times a day. And, of course, copious amounts of her homemade wine with a long skin contact. Specifically, the beautiful mtsvane, the Georgian grape grown on the eastern side of Georgia, honied and waxed.

About to land in Georgia for the first time, pushing through the white puffy clouds to land in Tbilisi before dawn, I felt its powerful vibration. Immediately upon walking around Tbilisi, I found the people familiar, as if I had known them for centuries. Their wine was a living tradition, like their language; their pride for it went deep. Their wines were unadorned simplicity packed with complexity, prophecy, and poesy. There was no celebration without wine. There was no death or birth without it. After the fall of communism, the children of those oppressed allowed themselves to dream of seeing their own names slapped onto the bottle. At first the home winemakers questioned whether the world would accept their ancient ways and were seduced into European grapes and technologies. But by 2011, there was the renaissance of pride in their traditional way of making wine in buried clay vessels, completely natural, and the white wine made with skin had texture and a sunlit amber color. In that year, there were five independent winemakers in the country staying true to their past. A decade later, the group had boomed to a force of more than a hundred and rapidly growing. The profession of those clay vessels for fermentation was saved from obscurity. It was as if all that energy had been trapped in a bottle for nearly a century. Once unleashed, the power was unstoppable, and that was all embodied in Lamara's wisdom.

Along with the cheesy pizzalike khachapuri, tomatoes, and cucumbers, and a cumin-heavy cabbage salad, Lamara brought out plastic pitchers of her chinuri. While she grew most of her own food, she bought her grapes, and of course, her wine was scratchy, amber-colored, deep, and beautiful.

I wished I could have shared this kaleidoscopic experience with my brother. I never thought that our last great time on the road would be that time we cleaned out Dad's apartment. It wasn't fair. So, on Andrew's last March on earth, I brought Georgia to him. We drank out of jelly glasses. High praise as he raised an eyebrow and said, "Not bad."

I told him how the wine was foot-stomped into a hollowed-out log and flowed with its skins and stems and seeds into a *qvevri* (an amphora but Georgian-style). The vessel was bulbous, with a point at the bottom, and buried in the ground up to its neck, and came in various volumes that ranged from reach-in-and-clean to jump-in-and-clean sizes. The red wine got moved off its skins after fermentation, usually after twenty-eight to thirty days. The white wine that was "skin contact" sat on the skins for up to eight months.

"Skin?" Andrew asked me.

"Most white grapes are immediately pressed off of their skins, and so the wines have no texture or color from the skins. The opposite of most reds. In Georgia, the white grapes are often made like red wines, with their skins. The skin makes the whites very ageable, and if the wines have no sulfur added, the skins give an antioxidant advantage."

I never told Andrew the whole story of Lamara. I never got to tell him how she finally married a man from her village with whom she had gone to school. How, at the time I met her in the hollow worm hut, her own brother was dying. I learned the history only years later, sitting on her porch after a *supra,* a Georgian feast, the dishes piled high on the table, as she joined her husband to smoke cigars and tell stories.

In the darkness by a table filled with goodness, Lamara said, "The worms can feel me when I come into the silk house. They get this excitement when they feel me. I learn from them, from their cycles, from their transformation and resurrection. When my brother died, a piece of me was cut off, and it was easier to keep the door closed. Working with the silkworms taught me about the rhythm of transformation. It helped me come to life again."

I did not have the silkworms to teach me any lessons. I'd have to find it another way. Maybe every time I take a sip of chinuri, there might be something else in there for me.

## DRINK THESE GEORGIAN WINES

Today you can find Georgians on some of the best wine lists in the world, from Denmark to Japan and the UK, France, and yes, the United States. The pocket-size country of Georgia is about the same size as West Virginia, yet it is packed with variety, almost six hundred indigenous grape varieties. Rkatsiteli and saperavi are the two most famous (chardonnay and cabernet equivalents). Some of the most commonly found others are takveri, chinuri, mtsvane, tsitska tsolikouri, kisi, and krakhuna. There is a wide variety of styles, so who cares if you can't pronounce mgaloblishvili or chkhaveri, just drink them.

### East Georgia

Here the climate is influenced by the desert, and the wines tend to be big-bodied and the skin-contact effect quite strong. The most common grapes for whites and ambers: chinuri, mtsvane, kisi. For reds: saperavi, shavkapito, tavkveri.

Look for these producers: Amor Mundi, GoGo (Ketevan Bereshvili), Artanuli Gvino (Khaka Bereshvili).

Pheasant's Tears (East and West), Tanini, Kortavebis Marani, (Tamuna Bidzinashvili), Iago's Winery, Marina's Wine, Okro's Wine, Chona's Marani, Mariam Iosebidze, Sister's Wines, Papari Valley, Lapati (sparkling wines), Iberieli (East and West), Natenadze Wine Cellar, Didgori Winemaking, Lagvinari, Zhuka-Sano Winery, Our Wine, Artanuli, Lagazi, Georgian Wine Foundation, Do-Re-Mi, Alpaiani, Kerovani

## West Georgia

The western part is wetter and cooler, with lighter wines, chuggable reds, and plenty of complexity. The most common white grapes are tsolikouri, krakhuna, and tsitska. For reds: chkhaveri, ojaleshi, and otskhanuri sapere. Look for these producers: Freya (Enek Peterson), Amiran Wine Cellar, Baia's Wine, Nino, Mariam Guniava's Winery, Achil Guniava's Wine Cellar, Nikoladzeebis Marani, Dato Chikhladze's Marani, Vino Martville, Kirile Marani, Perati, Makaridze Winery, Merab Ediberidze, Perati, Natenadze Wines, Didgori, Gvantsa's Wine, Oda Family Winery, Khvedeliani's Marani

# ROBERT'S DEAD TREE

Coming out of Union Station in downtown Los Angeles, I could feel the Mexican dust coating my hair and vineyard grit lining my nails. I got into the cab and said, "UCLA campus, please." Visibly grubby from travel, I'd need some time to scrub down in a shower before meeting the other presenters. But my cousin lived just a few minutes from the university. How could I be in his backyard and not at least knock on his door? What the hell, I said, blood over water. I quickly called to find out if I could stop by, "just to give you a hug," and changed the address of my destination.

Rolling my bag up to his modest stucco home—one of those petite Spanish-revival cottages—I stopped short, transfixed by a tragedy on his lawn. Stuck into his yard was a large tree, dead as driftwood. The soil beneath it had been drained of life. This fancy part of L.A. had gone through the process called desertification. Flora or human, you can't live without nutrition. I considered the lawn's past and that lifeless dirt. Sort of like a psychic, I could see its vivid tableau of years of irrigation with saline water, weed killers, and nitrogen-based nutrients. A negligent, unemphatic worker had killed off the living soil until it became sterile dirt. I stepped onto what I had presumed was once a lawn, yet the feeling under my sandals reminded me of my ass plopped on Ethel's old couch: The foam under its plush sunburned orange corduroy had hardened into rocks. The remarkable thing is, unlike humans or dead foam, soil can regenerate. If only I had a little time and some compost, I could resuscitate it.

Rob came out, his hand-crocheted *kippah* on his gray hair. I had last seen him when he flew to Milwaukee for my brother's funeral two years before. We had stood in pelting rain, tears streaming down our faces, shoes getting caked with the slick claylike mud as we took turns pitching dirt on the coffin. Now I ran to give him a hug. We both felt the memory but said nothing. As we pulled apart, I asked, "What's with the tree?"

"I don't know. A surgeon is coming to chop it up tomorrow," he replied.

I followed him into the house, thinking about our shared Brooklyn roots. The son of my mother's rabbi brother, Rob was a month older than my own brother. Andrew and Rob had grown up as close as twins. I adored him as well, my cool older cousin, a voracious reader, one time a Jerry Garcia look-alike who let me stay at his studio apartment in the city whenever I wanted.

But he had grown away from me by almost every measure. Religion, absolutely. Politics? Don't ask. Drinking? He had a migraine problem, so no alcohol. But we retained connection points—our love for my dead brother, and he was the only other writer in the family. For years, I'd longed for him to take me seriously, not just as his younger cousin but also as a colleague.

"So, what are you doing out here?" he asked, setting down an iced coffee in front of me.

"I was near Baja, checking out some vines."

"They have wine in Mexico?" he asked.

"Yup. But the reason I'm here," I proudly explained, "I'm speaking at something called the Urban Soil Summit."

"Whoa." He looked genuinely surprised. "Soil and you?"

Who could blame him? We grew up together. He knew me.

Soil and I had an unlikely history. As a pale redheaded yeshiva girl who could never tolerate being in the sun, I shunned the outdoors. I had no concept of a mountain. Volcanoes were only in picture and history books. The thought of camping nauseated me. Hiking put me in a bad mood. When I took geology in college, I flunked the course; it might as well have been calculus. Yet there I was, prepping to speak at the Urban Soil Summit.

"The theme is *terroir*," I said to him. "It's a term that is mostly associated with wine. I guess that's why they asked me." Knowing that most people don't really know what the word means, I did my best: "A French term that means more than earth. A combination of nature and nurture. Each plant has nature, but where it grows, and the way it is reared is its nurture. So a Red Delicious normally tastes different than a Macintosh. However, planting those varieties in New England and California, in disparate climates and soils, will produce even more variations on their taste. How you farm also makes a difference. If I have a plot of land planted to pinot noir, and on one half, I farm with chemicals, on the other, I farm without, and vinify in exactly the same way, the resulting wines will taste different. When something in wine is connected to a place, when it takes us somewhere, no matter whether we know where that place is, that is *terroir*. It's sort of like Roland Barthe's punctum, the 'accident which pricks me (but also bruises me, is poignant to me).'"

"Where we come from, our background, the influences that emotionally mark us. Our family. I get it," he said. "Cool. And what will you tell them?"

"I'm still not one hundred percent sure," I told him.

He raised his eyebrows. "You're just going to wing it?" he asked.

"No. No. I have a PowerPoint, of course," I said. But I didn't know what I could possibly tell a bunch of soil geeks that could be relevant. Just admitting that was enough to give me palpitations. I took a gulp of the coffee and called for a taxi.

As he walked me outside, he said, "Start off with Ethel. Trust me. Just find a way, and it will all flow from there."

"Make them laugh and they'll follow me anywhere? Spoken like a true screenwriter." I laughed, yet it stuck. What a way to start—tell them about a ninety-four-year-old woman who still commuted to New York City, unwilling to give in to old age? The one who couldn't understand why I couldn't have become a doctor like my brother or at least married one? Great idea, but unattainable.

I gave a nod of respect to the condemned tree and got into the car. On the way to the campus, my anxiety mounted. How did I come to accept that soil was miraculous? If I had to be honest about it, all roads led to the late nineties and a friend's Catskills bat-infested farmhouse that needed love and skilled hands. Sometimes at night, a group of us, actors and playwrights, lapsed or active, no matter what the weather, would gear up to withstand frigid cold. A geologist-freak actor friend would deliver lectures as we sat on large shale and slate slabs—how where we sat was once under the sea, how shale was formed of pressed mud and sand particles, and slate was shale metamorphized under pressure.

On one particular night, protected by long underwear and down, we sat high on the ridge in the expansive, remote field behind the house. While talking, we saw something glowing and throbbing under the frozen earth. "It's a glow worm?" I was filled with a sense of the miraculous. I placed my gloved hand over the spot as if I could feel its rhythm. "Nature is unstoppable," my friend said. That was the moment I understood that the soil never slept. Even in the dead of winter, there was life.

After that glimpse of the underworld, my connection to the soil was never the same. I finally absorbed on an emotional level what had been merely academic. Soil came to me surely but slowly, as if I could let in only a little bit at a time or my cranium would crack. Knowing that less than a teaspoon of healthy soil can hold up to one billion bacteria, several yards of fungal filaments, several thousands of microbes, and God knows what else could almost drive a girl like me to religion.

All of that was reconfirmed at the conference. I became an ardent fangirl of a woman pioneering regenerative fiber systems, finding ways to dye clothing without harming the universe. Listening to her talk about planting her used underwear so that they would return to the earth blew my mind. Biologists from Seattle who had converted right-wing midwestern farmers to farm less aggressively, convinced me that one step at a time might be a viable alternative to revolution. I learned how lucidly mycelia, the almost microscopic hairs in soil clumps, allow trees, and presumably vines, to communicate with each other.

I was at the back of the room, initially ready to leave to rehearse my presentation but I was stuck in my seat, pierced by a talk about the Montgomery, Alabama, museum commemorating the victims of lynching, the Memorial to Peace and Justice. The speaker showed a short, dramatic documentary that traced a California family's journey to the Southeast United States. We watched them surround a ghostly, bare tree and then shovel soil from its gnarly roots into a jar. That soil had borne witness to the lynching of their relative, Thomas Miles, in the 1800s. The project collected soils from nearly three hundred trees where men and women had been hanged. The soil specimens were jarred, named, and displayed at the museum. The silence in the room densely reflected this profound interpretation of *terroir*.

The film reminded me of a story told by a Georgian wine-maker and farmer. A colleague visiting him from another country had looked at his Pheasant's Tears vineyard and asked, "What kind of fertilizers do you use?"

"Fertilizers?" Gela had replied with a lack of patience. "This land is drenched with the blood of my ancestors. What do you use?" Every time Gela worked his land, he never lost sight of the kin whose dead bodies, snuffed out over centuries of war with the Turks and never-ending invaders, had nourished his land.

Images of the hardened mud on my shoes at my brother's grave, my cousin's tree, Gela's blood-soaked vineyards, and that soil-collection project left me overcome by exploding emotions. I was suddenly sick with fear. I wanted to pass a note to the organizer pleading a migraine and the need to retreat to bed. There was absolutely no way I could follow the journey of those three hundred jars of soil. My wine seemed trivial.

I closed my notebook and departed the auditorium and entered the bright California sunshine and heat. I sprinted around the building, talking to myself. I had two hours to come up with a plan. After two laps, I was out of breath. I stood in the shade, thinking, How can I communicate what I felt and saw under the parched Sierra Madres? The vines stood like trees, crazy with lots of flopping arms and leaves, their roots reaching down into sandy soil in pursuit of scarce water and nutrients. In the scratchy brush and dried grasses, I could hear the hissing of rattlers. That brutal landscape produced a wine so delicious that it was life-affirming, creating from adversity a blood-orange-like acidity and the silk-iness of the finest fabric. One sip transported me to that site. Each real bottle of wine can encapsulate its place and culture. Wine had that power. Yet how can that be communicated to a customer walking into a shop, asking for a cabernet under twenty dollars? Somehow it seemed senseless to me. Shouldn't customers be asking, "Show me a good story, I have up to twenty dollars to spend"?

"Start with your mother," cousin Robert had said. I headed back to my room, grabbed my computer, threw myself on the bed, and flew through my photos. There was the survivor vine, rising up to give fruit under the Sierra Madres. I found the photo of the wild and bee-filled vineyards in Georgia fertilized by ancestral blood. There was another shot from Chile and those pink granitic soils of Itata where Pinochet and the Mapuche's story was told through the local wines. Still trying to balance the sadness I felt from the lynching-tree presentation process, I found exactly the one picture of my mother I wanted. She was in her jewelry booth, her *terroir*, the only place she seemed to be at peace with the world, looking for a ring for a customer. I sent the pictures, with no captions, to my tech-savvy secret-weapon friend in Boston, who dumped them into the PowerPoint way more artistically than I ever could. "Your mother?" Liz asked me. "What she's doing in there?"

"Just do it, please."

I filed the presentation onto a thumb drive, returned to the auditorium, and gave it to the AV tech. I took the stage and looked at my audience, trying not to fidget or pass out.

"I have a mother," I began. "Not just any mother but a Jewish mother, and not just any kind of Jewish mother but *the* Jewish mother. I believe that if you look in the dictionary for a definition, you'll find her name, Ethel Feiring."

I clicked to her photograph. The room laughed loud and hard, out of fond recognition, not mockery. They loved Ethel in all her power and chutzpah. They knew her. Everyone had an Ethel somewhere in their *terroir*, who, though loving, made them feel maybe like they were not good enough. Those scientists and academics and ardent gardeners were with me. Never before had I understood what it meant to engage an audience. I felt high, emboldened.

"Here's the thing. She doesn't get me, and who can fault her? The closest she's ever gotten to digging in the soil was caring for a jade plant, and the nearest she's gotten to a fine wine was something that didn't come from a place but something called Mega Purple. And so is it any wonder that she looks at me with complete disappointment and says, 'This is what you do? Write about wine? This is important?'"

They roared.

I told them how the beauty of a grapevine is that it can grow where nothing else can. I relayed the adage: A vine that struggles makes the most beautiful of fruit. I showed them that treelike vine and a plant that had thrived in thirsty conditions for more than a century and, with the guidance of a farmer and winemaker, gave birth to something glorious. I cautioned that while the sun is essential, without topsoil and the rocks below, there can be no profundity. While wine can be seen as frivolous, it is actually the symbolic synthesis of our culture.

It hit me after that I wasn't talking to the audience, I was talking to Ethel, but the crowd was with me, and charged with their energy, I soared. I'm sure I will never be able to pull off that kind of performance again, but that moment onstage was intoxicating. I might have hit the stage feeling as fearful as Robert's tree was dead, but like soil, I regenerated.

## DRINK THIS

Agricola Macatho
Segundo Flores
Grape: País
Where: Maule Valley, Chile

From the village of Pilen (place of the fog) comes this lovely smoky país. Yes, this particular one was affected by the local fires in that year, but it didn't matter that it reminded me of an Islay Scotch with a fresh snappy plumminess. Somehow it all worked. Bitter cherry and silk made for a complementary addition to the mix, with remarkable acidity, born of those red granite, red clay, and schist. Nostalgia of oranges? Yes, that mandarin just lingered in my mouth, as if imprinting the flavor in my memory forever.

I was trailing winemakers Macarena and Thomas up a steep hill. Maca was a skilled forager. She kept on shoving leaves at me to chomp on—furry melissa, earthy thymes, and icy mints. She snapped off a mandarin orange from a century-old tree, and its flavor popped so that I actually saw colors. All around us, wild vines raced up the trees. This was early summer in Chile. I had come here to do a story on the revival of the old grape, país. My journey led me to this young winemaking couple in the remote mountain village Pilen and a wine named after its recently deceased farmer, Segundo Flores. We had just left the blood-rose-red geranium-festooned adobe hut of Segundo's ninety-year-old widow, an abode where the chickens had free range.

Pilen was said to be a once-thriving village known for its women potters and its spectacular vineyards. Today it's population is practically vanishing. In 1973 Segundo's daughter, a teacher, had 160 students in the school. Today there are none. The men and the young either moved away to get jobs or died off, like Segundo. While Maca and Thomas long to farm, they are blessed to be able to buy the fruit for now, and it is that lone man on the mountain, Segundo's cousin, who is in charge of the vineyard.

The vineyard has three beautiful chambers with graceful, crawling vines of país, pressing their roots deeply into the red granitic soils of this biodiverse environment. The bees were so contented that I never once worried about stings. Now, I thought, this, this was a place.

Nature offers up some undeniable truths. One of them is that with two adjacent pieces of land, farmed using the same practices, one can prove better than the other. Each location hosts its own microclimate shaped by local patterns of wind and weather. This is what I mean by *terroir*, that ultimate compliment you can give to a wine.

Before I visited this part of Chile, I was struck by wines that came from the mysterious place called Pilen. True, I had tasted only two of them, but they spoke to me. I felt I had to go there and seek the truth. It was as if the wines had lassoed my waist and pulled me to the slopes among the país that grew there.

País arrived in South America from the Canary Islands in the 1500s with the conquistadors (one had to be ready to plant vines: Wine was a necessary aspect of life). From there it spread out to North America, where at one time it was the most wildly planted grape in California. But the grape, used mostly for sacramental wine, developed a bad reputation, and cabernet took over. Today only a few acres remain. The unfairly maligned grape seems to have maintained its fine reputation only in Spain, on the island of Tenerife. Yet it was beloved in Chile for centuries and made an easy-to-drink country wine called Pipeño.

The grape's stature was diminished in the 1800s when Chile fell in love with varieties from France and rejected the Spanish ones. When Pinochet came to power in 1973, he modernized Chile's wine world. The shift made a lot of people rich but decimated the historical winemaking in the country. He encouraged ripping out old and beautiful vines and offered farmers money to plant non-native trees for the paper industry. As a result, much of the beautiful muscat and país vines were ripped out. Some Pinochet-era enologists claimed that the grape responsible for Pipeño produced a "brown and thin wine." Others called Pipeño a raw wine that "has all the impurities, called borras or feces."

The grape and the wine, what was left of it, were reduced to a sentimental choice. It was a wine that grandfathers might remember from their grandfather. A wine that brought someone back to the romance of the country, when life was simpler, but not something to show the guests.

This was a viticultural tragedy. As one winemaker had told me, "Give país even a little love and it loves you back." It was so easy to see why: Drink them and you too will feel loved. Finding "Quilmo," a poem by 1950s poet Raúl Rivero, I smiled contentedly as I read, "Pipeño, clear, flavored nostalgia or oranges." There you go. The poet's favorite wine brought him to a place, to a memory. But it is far, far more than nostalgia. The wine is history, and respect and love can make a wine indeed fit for guests.

We stood on top of the mountain, looking down at the vines. This was not my first time at a vineyard rodeo, so I always try to palpate its story from the field or drink the fruit of its labors. The vineyards don't have to be beautiful. Well, they're never ugly unless they've been abused, but some are harsh and stark, like that Mexican vineyard with the rattlers ticking in the grass. The wine from that spot told a story of struggle, and yet the wines were a marvel. There are some Vermont wines more than others in which I can absolutely sense the chill air and the ramp-riddled crystal brooks in Vermont. When I taste some rkatsiteli from eastern Georgia, I can sense the nearby desert. On the west coast of Imereti, with certain wines I can feel the wormwood and bees. No matter where I am, when I taste a wine that moves me, I feel the imperative to follow the thread to its origin, and that's when I know I've got something special. I knew it as I stood on the mount, dwarfed in the shadows of the Andes.

We sat in the vines and looked down on the Maule. We

talked about the decades wasted using technology to produce too many impersonal wines while doing everything possible to irradicate país and any sense of the wine's place. Now país was back.

Maca took out a quinoa salad. We savored *humitas* picked up in the nearby Cauquenes market, where women from this village still sat on blankets hawking their clay pots. Wine glasses and two vintages of the Segundo came out. One from 2017. That year the wildfires came through on the taste and smell, yet underneath the char was the subtle cherry. So lovely. The 2018, not yet ready, was smoky just from the fruit and brighter. Sitting there in the middle of the vines and sipping wine in that paradise, with the biodiversity all around us, I thought of Segundo and how he must have held on to his land while Pinochet was handing out money to peasant farmers. I imagine that Segundo said no. No one was going to mess with his país and his Pilen.

There was a large fallen tree nearby. I asked about it and Maca told me proudly, "It was the only eucalyptus here. Thomas and I chopped it down." Maca might have been as slim as a teenager, but she was warrior powerful. This patch of earth was capable of birthing a wine of beauty. The fruits of that vineyard resulted from someone who stitched a royal diamond into his farmer's rags. Even in death, Segundo, a man I had never met, had put his soul into the earth and what it gave.

## DRINK THESE PAÍS

Some people think país (or any of its other names; misión, mission, rosa del Peru, or listán prieto) originated in the

Sherry region, but it flourished in the Canaries, and that was its link to the Americas. Wherever you pick yours up, the wine can be seen in a light quaffable wine or a dense serious one, but often like smoked blueberries. It has a serious affinity for high altitude and granite soil.

Chile: Cacique Maravilla, A Los Viñateros Bravos, Roberto Henriquez, El Viejo Almacén de Sauzal, Louis-Antoine Luyt, Viña Gonzáles Bastías, Tinto de Rulo, Agricola La Misión, Garage Wine Co.

Mexico (misión, rosa del Peru): Bichi Winery, La Casa Vieja

Canary Islands (listán prieto): Envínate

Argentina (criolla chica): Catena Finca Los Paraísos, El Mirador, Cara Sur

# LOOSE ENDS

On Friday morning of Labor Day weekend, my brother had run out of options. It was clear that he would be actively dying very soon. I was in such a state I was unable to do much other than pace. Impending deadlines did me no good because I kept doing laps from my apartment's stem to stern. There was no way I could sit down long enough to slap words on a page. As the minutes ticked, my list of ailments grew. I thought, Okay, give my mother's old advice a shot, "When in despair, go shopping." Perhaps I could push myself into denial by overfocusing on something in my budget: socks and cotton underwear at Century 21.

Before I left the apartment, I had some inexplicable impulse: I swapped out my usual eyeglasses for the wire-rims of my teen years. I must have felt some primal need for a time when life seemed possible. I locked the door, then was struck by panic: What if I bumped into someone I knew? I returned home and quickly swiped a rust red on my lips. I locked the door and tromped down the green steps. On the second floor, I realized I'd forgotten my wallet. Back up the stairs, in the door, I grabbed it and went back down and headed to the downtown subway.

Once I was floating up the store's escalator, seeing earnest shoppers with their full baskets of merch made me feel even more angry and helpless. My hurt was too expansive. It was no use. How could I be so shallow? How could I look to escape? Feeling shame for my weakness, I ran down the up escalator and out to Broadway to walk north. Some pains, I said to myself, must be absorbed until they burst, and healing commenced. I was so very far from the commencement.

I talked to the universe for the entire two-mile walk back to my neighborhood and took the right off Broadway onto Prince. As I passed the window of McNally Jackson Books, I caught a glimpse of myself in my uniform-like Uniqlo blue-and-white-striped seersucker dress and flat utilitarian leather sandals. My fading-to-pink red hair was pinned up because it was so humid. Frumpy, I thought, and turned away from my reflection and once again argued with God, beseeching the deity to reverse my brother's death. In midsentence, just in front of the bookstall outside the bookstore, a man jumped, lynxlike, into my path. He startled me, pointed his index finger in my face, and stated with the confidence of getting the answer right on *Jeopardy!,* "Alice Feiring."

My brain tried to Google-search for his name. His hair was silvery. He was lean, handsome. I knew those dark, chipmunklike, close-set eyes. But at book events and talks, I meet so many people. Could he be a fan? No. I liked his face with its playful resemblance to Frank Zappa's. I knew him. Somewhere in the past, there was love for him.

"Peter," he told me.

I threw my arms around him. I squeezed my eyes. This was miraculous. The crush of my youth, the older boy from across the street where we lived, my brother's long-lost friend, just stops me on the street on one of the worst days of my life. But I could feel him tense up under my hands. I withdrew my tentacles and tried not to be embarrassed by my enthusiasm.

"How did you ever recognize me?" I said, stepping back to examine him, but almost like he was a phantom.

"Well, your hair is still red," he said, smiling shyly.

I was eighteen the last time I saw him, and he was twenty-seven, living and working in the city at the radical listener-sponsored radio station WBAI, the only station I listened to, a lifeline. He had just driven from New York to visit his parents and change his car's oil. His long, thick, dark ponytail squiggled down to his waist. Finally, fully legal, I'd flirted with as much might as I could muster. I was so smitten. I remembered how he looked, his hand pushing against his 1960 Citroën D1, as he'd told me his Saab story. I laughed at his punning. He was flirting with me too. And yet he was leaving. I asked, "Are you coming back?"

"Yes," he promised, "I'll come back."

Remembering that moment I asked him, "What took you so long?" I asked now, thinking that Ulysses only made Penelope wait twenty years. It had taken Peter forty.

"So, I'm a little late," he admitted, looking me in the eye. He remembered too.

The trio of men he had been walking with stopped talking among themselves and turned their eyes on us. Feeling their pressure, Peter said, "Tell me how to find you, so I don't lose you again."

"So I don't lose you" replayed in my ears. Not leaving any of this to faith—I was too old for that—I took out my phone, asked for his email, and connected us the modern way. This time he hugged me back. I thought maybe it was true that he was afraid of losing me. I was surprised that he didn't ask me about my brother, but I was grateful, because if I had blurted out, "He's dying," I wouldn't have been strong enough to see his reaction without crumbling.

If I'd told him what Andrew and I had done just two weeks before, he might have felt terrified, maybe even stalked. In the most recent visit to Milwaukee, while Andrew's wife conversed with my mother, my brother and I talked of Peter, how they fingerpicked together, leaving me far in the dust when it came to guitar playing. My technique was never as good as theirs. Andrew said, "Pull out that laptop, let's find him." The two of us went at it. We even searched in obituaries. "He has no footprint," I said. "He's undiscoverable. How, in 2013, can you not leave an Internet trail?"

"Well," Andrew adroitly said, "he probably never stopped being paranoid and covers his tracks. When he grew up, it was dangerous to be communist."

As a little kid, I'd thought Peter's family, in the house near Grand Avenue with Tyrone, the horny Labrador, were merely different. If I had been old enough, though, I'd have caught the signs that he and his brother were true Red Diaper babies. At eleven, I failed to understand the significance when Peter's family gave my brother art books and a Pete Seeger album for his bar mitzvah instead of cash. My mother, however, glibly said, "Of course they were Communists. Rose [Peter's mother] never went to the beauty parlor."

They must have felt so out of place on our block full of conventional Democrats. No wonder Andrew and I were so drawn to them.

My steps home were adrenalized as I thought, Peter in my neighborhood? On my turf? At the moment when I needed him the most? As soon as I shut the door behind me, I texted my brother: "I just ran into Peter!"

A second later, the phone rang. "That is spooky," Andrew said and for a moment, we both forgot he was dying as he launched into the questions: "Does he still play?"

"I don't know, we just had a ten-minute conversation."

"Is he still in radio?"

"I have no idea."

"Does he still have hair?"

That I could answer: "Yes! But it's short and very white. Kind of like his mother's."

"Is he married?" Andrew asked.

"I don't think he is."

He paused. "Is this going romantic?"

"That can't be avoided."

"Well, when will you see him?"

"He'll have to call me first."

Andrew had never been so interested in any man I'd been with. Stephen? Eh. Herb? Oh, God. Ronny? Disdain would not have been too strong a word. But Peter was personal to him. I had the inescapable feeling that somehow Andrew had plucked Peter out of the past and pasted him into my present. There was no logical explanation for how he'd appeared in that moment of all moments. Nor was there any true reason why I'd grabbed the round wire-rims, the very ones I'd worn when we had last seen each other. My hair was red, and I was wearing the same glasses. He recognized me. Sometimes one can blame too much on coincidence. The kismet was almost enough to make a religious woman out of me.

I craved the sky and space, so I grabbed a seltzer and walked up the splintering stairs to the roof. I gave the paint-chipped door a shove, and then I was out. In the air. I tried to take a deep breath. I walked to the front that overhung the street and scanned the water towers punctuating my little skyline and the skyscraper going up into the air where the World Trades used to be. Bad and beatific angels were battling for my soul. How could I possibly be falling in love just as I was bracing myself for terrible grief. How can those two feelings occupy the same moment and the same heart.

I unearthed my earliest Peter memories. Had I really met him as a four-year-old and played with his electric trains? I could visualize his mother in her housedress and anklets at the spinet. Damn Tyrone, that black Lab who terrorized my leg, always following me to hump it. I had vague memories of sitting on a chair in the garage while Peter reconstructed and connected wires on his short-wave radio. By the time I was fifteen, Peter was coming back to visit on his motorcycle. "Peter! Please take me for a ride, please," I begged him.

"You'll have to ask your mother."

He blew it. He totally blew it. I was so upset: With his long hair, he was supposed to be a rebellious bad boy. But up there on the rooftop, as people cleared out for the long weekend below, something else was going on besides my consideration of Peter's character. Before this afternoon, I had arrived at a peace with being single. It had been several years since I'd had a serious relationship. I had decided I was giving up, because men my age were too old and younger men were far too young. I would rather spend time with my friends and travel than spend time searching for magic. I was officially content with that decision.

Peter's return shook all of my fine convictions. On top of

that, he was Jewish. After years of serial monogamy, here was one man I could finally take home to Mom.

He didn't call. Two weeks later, I gave in. I chose a Friday because that was when he was downtown lunching with his buddies. I wrote, "Why don't you come over early evening? We'll catch the sunset from my roof and what do you like red or white?'

I fretted, but this time he didn't make we wait. I got such an enthusiastic response I was confused—what had he been waiting for? We did not have another forty years to bump into each other again. He arrived, we talked until dusk when I suggested I pull together some dinner. I just remember walking past him as he sat at the head of the table. I can still feel his arm swooping me into his lap, the smoothest dance move ever.

The second time we got together was the night before I flew to Tbilisi to do some last-minute research and meet with Stalin's last winemaker. Peter had told me he had a bottle stashed away. "Do you like Barolo?" he asked.

Barolo? Old Barolo? How did he know? He told me that the wine had been sleeping in his closet ever since he was given the bottle as a gift. I did the math: about the same year I moved back to New York City from Boston. It was a 1981 Vietti, from the time the winery was still old world and exalted (in my eyes). It was the last year the wine was made from old vines of the now impossible to find nebbiolo rosé. Vietti had purchased the grapes, and a year or two after this bottle was made, the owner replated the vineyard with far inferior grape vines, I can only imagine because the light-color and lighthearted wines were falling out of fashion. The back of the label said drink between four and ten years. There we were, drinking it more than thirty years later, and my eyelids fluttered; I was speechless. The wine was pale garnet, fragile, yet electric with crushed rose petals. It was a whisper and a secret, but most significantly, that bottle was the Cinderella's slipper.

Later, with my head on Peter's chest as if it belonged, his arms around me as if they were glued, I asked him what he remembered about me. "You were very quiet, and you were very pretty. You were never Andrew's annoying little sister." He finally asked about Andrew, and I told him. "I'll help you through this," he said. I knew he would, even if it was his comforting silence filling the room.

Only three weeks later, it was Andrew's endgame. On that trip out I sat at his feet waiting for the lucid moments. He heroically tried to pull out of his medicated haze to connect, but often failed. I got up. I sat down. I got up and circled back to Andrew's bed. I laid my hand on his arm and put my head very near his, conscious that I needed to imprint his smell forever. I held him, something I'd never done, and he let me. As kids, we horsed around. We read side by side, and he'd drop his leg on me like a log. We'd play guitar. He'd tease me and punch me, damn, it hurt. His skin felt impressionable, like when I bake bread and I press into the pillowy dough. "I don't want to go," I said to him, trying to paint those last moments into my brain so I'd have them forever.

Very lucidly, he replied, "I know. I know. But you have to." Then for the first and last time, he told me he loved me, then he asked me about Peter. It was the one loose end that needed tying up.

## DRINK THIS

Giovanni Scanavino
Barolo
Grape: Nebbiolo
Where: Piemonte, Italy

This purloined bottle was fraught with parental conflict and guilt. Yet it is the one wine that took me through the looking glass. Scanavino had a sketchy reputation, but this was the year he shone. He bought the grapes from a vineyard right on the very hill of Barolo. Drunk in its twelfth year, it smelled like rose petals left in the back of a hot car; it went down with suedelike tannins, beach tar, and black tea. Whenever I taste a rare wine like that, and it happened when I drank the 1981, I go back to that moment of contemplation and discovery and wonder: Why does Barolo and its grape, nebbiolo, follow me wherever I go?

I knew what I was doing was wrong, neither moral nor ethical. A bottle of Barolo in my hand, I felt like a jewelry thief, waiting for the cops to bust me. Instead, I heard Phyllis's kittenlike purr call out from the kitchen, "Take it all."

An hour before, I was just a normal girl reluctantly paying her father a visit on Long Island. At that point, my parents had been divorced for eight years. I had fled to Cambridge, Massachusetts. Mom had migrated to Long Beach. And Dad was living with Phyllis in the Baldwin house she previously shared with her husband, Arthur. Phil, Phyllis, and Arthur. What a trio they were. Arthur, an orthodontist, often joined them for dinner or brunch. He still had his office in the house and, as I found out, that wine cellar. "You're learning about wine?" Phyllis asked, a bit as if I'd told her I'd taken up skydiving. "Did you know Arthur is obsessed? You should see him drink. First he swirls the wine like this"—she imitated with a careful rotation of her martini glass—"then he smells it, then he gargles with it. It's too much, don't you think?" Then she took a sip of gin.

There was a plate of taut green and black grapes on the table, marinated artichokes and almonds in adorable, petite, hand-painted bowls from their recent trip to Tuscany. Including the overlap with my parents' marriage, my dad and Phyllis had been together just over sixteen years. Yet visiting them still made me feel on edge and my stomach queasy.

"But really," Dad asked, "what is there to know about wine?"

"I'm not studying," I said. "It's more like drinking and exploring."

That was when Phyllis told me about the wine cellar. "Arthur built it when the kids were little," she said, and I did the calculation, late sixties, when the only alcohol I knew was my father's beer and my mother's Manischewitz. "Take a look. If you see something you want, take it!" Phyllis fluffed her pixie haircut with her fingers, her gold hoops glinting under the kitchen light.

My father scratched his goatee and took a big toke of his smelly pipe. I coughed and waved the smoke away. "*Per favore*, Mouse, go ahead," my father said.

Phyllis was always lecturing me about women's liberation (she whom two men supported). Now she was asking me to steal.

"I can't do that," I said, feeling myself flush.

"Don't be silly. Call it rent for keeping the bottles here; he was supposed to take them years ago."

Color me curious. Giving in, I followed her to a human-size cat door off the kitchen. She flicked the switch. "Have fun," she said.

I lowered to my knees and snaked myself in. Only five feet, I still couldn't stand to my full height. As my eyes adjusted to the yellow-hued light, I saw maybe a hundred filthy bottles. What a dumb place to keep wine, I thought. Wine needed to be kept cool, preferably closer to fifty-five. That cubbyhole, which had to have been in the high seventies, was nowhere close to ideal.

"Clean it out!" my father's woman shouted from the kitchen.

There were many wines I'd seen on supermarket shelves, like Hearty Burgundy from Gallo and low-cost Germans like Liebfraumilch. Even through the Germans' green bottles, I could tell what was inside had turned color and evaporated. Beginner's mistake number one: Not every wine is ageable.

Most will go south after a couple of years. What makes a wine capable of a long life that grows older and wiser? There are some benchmarks for success: grown well from a talented piece of land, with enough tannin that can transform and deepen into a kind of sweetness and enough acid to hold the fruit. Put all of those together and there you go, potential. But even to my barely educated assessment, half of what the orthodontist had bought seemed ready for the drain.

I swept the gritty mold from the labels, rejected one, picked up another. The pressure was on with the cheerleading on the other side of the wall. I persisted in hunting and eventually slid out a cruddy bottle with a scratched-away label. Mice?

The wine was from Italy, the country that delighted my father. When he and Phyllis came back from their long vacation there, he started to slip *"grazie"* and *"per favore"* into conversation any way he could. It was a little difficult to read the label. I rubbed more dirt away and sighed with defeat because I knew, though it felt unseemly to accept her gifts, I had found the one bottle I couldn't resist. A Barolo, a legendary wine. A long hauler. Ageable. Supposedly the real thing. I'd never had one. "I guess I do have a price tag," I said to myself. "It's called a twelve-year-old Barolo." The wine was a 1968 Giovanni Scanavino Barolo.

When I emerged, I felt like that bottle and I were as soot-covered as Phyllis's words were sugar-coated.

"Just one?" she asked. "When someone says take, take!"

"I never should have named you Mouse," my father said through another puff of smoke. "You've become one."

I was twenty-five years old. They saw I was hopeless.

Later at LaGuardia, I stashed the Barolo in my bag and

found my seat on that nineteen-dollar People Express flight to Boston. My boyfriend, Stephen, met me at Logan. He didn't drink, but the following weekend, we invited friends over for dinner who did. One of them had a serious wine cellar of mostly Italian wines, and I looked to him to explain the wine to me, should I need it. We all need a guide, and at the time, he was mine. Over ravioli from the North End and smoked mozzarella from Al Capone's, we had that 1968 Giovanni Scanavino.

My wine friend could tell me the basics. There were eleven communes in the Piemonte region and five major ones that could be labeled Barolo: La Morra, Castiglione Falletto, Monforte d'Alba, Serralunga d'Alba, and the town that is called Barolo. At the time, all those wines were raised up in big old barrels; the wines needed their time and were considered unapproachable—too young. For me, tasting it was love at first sight, something I understood. I rarely did it any other way. Wines, I found, were like people. If you listen carefully, you hear what you need to know in those first few minutes. That Barolo showed me that wine could be something more than a drink, than a buzz. It could stir my fantasies and hopes and raise goose bumps.

What was the attraction? Everything. The Barolo's aromas and tastes of hot rose petals. There was a bit of gravel and tar and tea. There was a touch of limelike sumac. There was tannin which, in my mouth, made me remember a suede vest that I loved to touch but could never bring myself to wear. In 1980, that Barolo was a preteen, but with those tannins, it had already grown up gorgeous. Later on, I'd find out that these were classic aromas and tastes, you read these words in all the wine books, but I didn't need anyone to tell me it was phenomenal. I figured it out with my own nose. From then on, I never looked at wine in the same way.

Barolo has stayed with me, even though it came from the hands of a woman I wish I could forget. Just how much impact did that bottle and Phyllis have on my life? I've been asking myself that question for decades. When my father finally left her five years later, he told me, "You were right, she was mean." But if my father had stayed with my mother, would I have found wine in the same way? Intentional or not, the woman and her effect on my life haunt. So does the wine. From crappy Manischewitz to filched Barolo is not everyone's journey, but it was mine.

## DRINK THESE LANGHE NEBBIOLO

When it comes to this region in Italy's northwest territory, I'm like a local dog with a Piemontese white truffle: all-consumed, obsessed, and hormonally activated.

Northern Italy is nebbiolo's home region. Whether from Alto Piemonte, Donnas, Carema, or Valtellina (which might have been its origin), the ones from the Langhe are considered the most royal. This is where Barolos and Barbarescos, neighboring regions, are situated. Those holy of holies are made from the same grape and yet separated by soil type and geography. Taste-wise, they are quite similar, and I can't tell you one is better than the other; it depends on producer and vineyard location. But both have become quite expensive. As climate change progresses, the wines become riper and less elegant, yet greatness can still be found.

By local law, Barbaresco must be aged at least two years before release, and nine months of that have to be done in oak.

Barolo laws require three years before being released, with a year and a half in oak. If you see a label that has "Riserva" on it, that means the producers had to age the wines even longer before releasing them. Even then they probably need more aging in your home before you pop them. The wines are between medium- and full-bodied and often muted in the smell category unless they acquire some age; then you get the rose in a clay pot, some licorice and sandalwood. These are serious ones for the table, not just cracking open when the guests come in. The most perfect combination is actually with expensive white truffles, but it's also delicious with humble cheesy pastas, mushrooms, and smoked things. If you want some nebbiolo goodness but can't find a properly aged Barolo or want something less expensive, get a wine that is simply labeled nebbiolos from a great producer. The wine will have some of the similar flavors but just a little less, shall we say, ponderous. And easy to drink within five years (or more) of its vintage date. All producers of Barolo and Barbaresco make one. So hunt them down.

Barolo: Cappellano, Ferdinando Principiano, Giuseppe Rinaldi, Flavio Roddolo, Roagna, Brovia, Giovanni Canonica, Lorenzo Accomasso, Bartolo Mascarello, Scarpa, Poderi Colla, Cacina Disa, Carlo Viglione, Trediberri

Barbaresco: Roagna, Cascina delle Rose, Ca' Nova, Roccalini, Fabio Gea, Produttori del Barbaresco, Olek Bondonio

# THE ANGST AND ANXIETY
# OF DRINKING ALONE

Sixty days into our lockdown, on a Friday night at six-fifteen, my boyfriend, Peter, called, and I couldn't bring myself to answer the phone, so I let it ring. I felt incapable of talking. I didn't want to tell him what I was planning to do. "Desperate times require desperate measures," I quipped to myself, and got down on my knees to fish behind the bottles of olive oil I kept in my cupboard. There it was. I pulled out the jar containing the psylocibin a friend had slipped me a year before. "Want these?" she'd asked. "I'm not going to use them."

Well, I surely wasn't going to look the gift horse in the mouth. One day, I thought, they might come in handy. The instinct within me was that those shriveled-up caps and stems would be my salvation.

Back in the early days of quarantine, I hadn't even remembered I had the mind-benders, as my focus was elsewhere. In those days when the sun went down and the streets of New York were hauntingly, terrifyingly silent, I found myself resisting the persistent whisper—"Time for a drink"—that often came far too early. By my self-made regulations, I pulled out the corkscrew only when powering down my computer for the day; this could be late, and I might also be hungry. As my soup was simmering—there was always soup—I'd survey the bottle options. Of course, there were plenty to choose from.

When the shelter-in-place order was issued, I scrambled to stock up with as much wine as I could afford. Now that there were no public tastings and I couldn't travel every month, as I was used to, I had to find new wines for the recommendations that others relied on me for. To be completely clear, I was not solely motivated by my professional obligation. This shopping spree was personal: Having a full house was going to be a major source of comfort. Fortification was necessary in the face of the unknown. A sea of bottles from the world over soon cluttered the bench in my living room, were stuffed into cubbyholes in my bedroom, and were loaded into the two pint-size, double-decked thermo-electric fridges near my desk. Even I had to admit I was at saturation point.

Given my own response, and everyone elses it seemed, wineshops were surely essential businesses. When Nielsen reported U.S. sales of alcoholic beverages were skyrocketing and that wine sales were up 66 percent over the same time the previous year, I nodded. How could it be otherwise? There was a time not too long ago when wine and booze were medicinal, often safer to drink than water. Even if it didn't work out that way, as Camus said in the more-prescient-than-ever *The Plague,* "Protection against infection was a good bottle of wine." With COVID coming for us, we needed all the immunity wine could give.

When drinking with others (even one other), my game plan had always been to choose specific wines to oil the joints of conversation, wit, gossip, and sometimes argument. I loved to pour from magnums—double the normal size of bottles—because they were more festive and more people could share in the same experience without bottle variation. But when people were getting sick, dying, in abject misery and fear, fancy and expensive options seemed obscene. So, fully expecting Peter to bunk in with me during quarantine, I selected a broad spectrum to cover all needs and moods, glou-glou, savory, tannic but fun, sparkles. Nothing fancy. And no big bottles, as there were to be no crowds. However, I hadn't foreseen one particular glitch: It wasn't going to be "ours" and "we." Peter, who saw COVID as certain death, decided to decamp and shelter in his own home ten miles north. While this was probably wise, I felt wounded and suddenly, inconsolably, on my own.

As a writer, I'm regularly in need of solitude. If I don't have enough solitude, I turn tart and nasty. I need to fret and pace and think with no distraction. I never had a problem with solo drinking. Assessing wines, with multiple bottles open, tasting and spitting, by myself, was often a daily affair. When alone for dinner, I never abstained; food tasted better with a glass and sometimes even three. The buzz was part of the charm, but it was rarely the point. When drinking alone (a silly social taboo), I have always had an established guideline to keep me on the correct side of tipsy. It could not be expensive, irreplaceable, or so profound that I would be made sadder by having no one to share it with. I also cut myself off at half a bottle, remembering to never cross the line from comforting to numbing. I loved being able to drink, and I would not abuse the privilege.

Over those unsettling weeks, as I got used to a cavelike living in my flat, something went screwy with my palate. Nothing tasted as it should; the wines were too tannic, too fruity, too metallic. I knew that anosmia, the inability to taste or smell, a wine writer's nightmare, was one of COVID's first symptoms. For nights on end, I panicked. Had the disease come for me? Without the taste buds and nose that had fueled my life, without my tools, my avocation would be over, and so would my livelihood. I envisioned myself thirsty and homeless. If I did get sick, who would take care of me? And who would take care of my mother? Having lectured her that COVID for a ninety-six-year-old would be a sure and nasty death, I finally got her to hand over the car keys (long overdue). The downside was that I was in charge of driving out to Long Beach weekly to make sure she didn't starve and to monitor her health.

In a panic, I freely popped bottles, looking for one that would give me the desired deliciousness, show me I was healthy. I was like a mathematician chewing over a singular problem, trying to come up with the right quotient. I opened another bottle and another. But nothing worked.

I knew that it wasn't the virus, I hadn't been near anyone to get it. But I also knew that I was fooling myself. In all the years of thinking I was perfectly happy to drink alone, I hadn't appreciated that this scenario was a novelty to me. So much of my work life was nocturnal. After a day of solitude, come eight p.m. everything changed: I met visiting winemakers, met with colleagues, opened bottles, explored new wine bars. Having a night to myself was a rarity. When the opportunity did come, I had a welcome evening of solitude and personal recharge. The coronavirus lockdown's imposed social isolation offered me my first experience of an extended time of drinking without community, friends, partners, or colleagues. Without Peter. What was left was me and the bottle and not even a dog around to ask, "What do you think?"

Zoom sessions were nice in a pinch, but they were awkward and didn't allow for the shared emotional moment, watching wine evolve and shape-shift. For me, wine met its match in captivity. Wine needed people.

As day eight segued to day thirty-five, my loneliness started to transmogrify into something physical. It was as if I were wearing a scratchy wool sweater under my flesh. I exercised, fretted, and drank more, for effect and not experience. I still was deriving no delight from wine and found myself landing on sherry, which at the time seemed less wine and more stone. It was not fragrant and was plenty salty. The wine became medicine. I called a nearby shop for emergency rations.

In the light of growing depression, so much for my rules. I knew that my grip on pleasure had loosened after my brother's death seven years before; listening to music became almost unbearable. That grief was compounded by an unfortunate brush with cancel culture and my own cancer diagnosis months in the fall of 2019. While both resolved with time and surgery, the experience was so intense that I couldn't talk about it without stuttering. Those were the seeds of misery that germinated for me in the too loud silence of the coronavirus era. And with not being able to feel wine, something that had sustained me through most of my life, I had no more threads connecting me to the ground. Fearing that I would lose myself down the rabbit warren of anhedonia or worse, I retrieved that trippy stash from behind my vinegars and oils.

I weighed the mushrooms out to 1.5 grams on my handy bread scale.

Nibbling those papery-dry brown caps and skinny ashy stems, I found them far more pleasant than I remembered. I wondered for a second if they were just enoki and not the hallucinogenic kind. Just in case they were potent, I set some goals. I wanted to reacquaint myself with the sensuality of wine. I wanted to open a few bottles and let them take me to the reason this agricultural product had dominated my life. While I was listening for wine, I needed to reclaim music. The two were connected.

Remembering how the senses were sharpened under

the influence, I darkened the apartment and set candles in strategic positions through the house. At seven p.m., I had my first shivers: It seemed that the fungi were not enokis. The light turned blue. I pulled out Beethoven's Op. 131 in C-sharp minor and swaddled myself on the bed. Having no idea how strong my experience would be, I needed to be prepared. The cello, mournful, pulled at something in me. I segued to *Goldberg Variations,* choosing Glenn Gould's earliest recording. Had I ever really felt the genius of Bach? I knew the enormity of his powers, but no other human could create voices like he did, and just then Gould's mutterings behind the notes came at me with clarity. He was pulling my tendons like a banjo's strings.

On to Mozart. Oh dear, that was a mistake. So tinkly, banal. Please no, I thought. I loved Mozart and feared I'd never be able to listen to *The Magic Flute* again. Whether or not I perceived the commerciality of the opera, I was definitely getting used to that music thing and could feel a touch of peach color stirring within me. But since it was just like me to seek out the black lining in every cloud, I put on Dylan's "Boots of Spanish Leather." My cheeks were soaked as I remembered the man who first played it for me, urging me to swim past the ropes with him. I was being ambushed, but that was the point. I needed to be ambushed, to get rid of my crust, to feel new skin.

Jimi's "Drivin' South." I blasted many variations from bootleg recordings, dancing through my apartment with abandon, punching the air, pulling out my seams. I jumped until I dripped sweat, with all the energy a touch of magic could give. Exhausted, I looked up to the clock in my kitchen. I had been at it for four hours. I wasn't hungry, but I could imagine drinking. Which one would it be?

The last time I had tripped completely alone, I was seventeen. Forty-five years later, I ingested for the same reasons. A depth of loneliness and pain, a desire to examine, understand, and fix. While drinking is linked with sociability, for me, eating mushrooms was always about the inward excursion for discovery. As I looked at the bottles I had preselected, I heard my mother tell me, "Great love only happens in novels." I'd heard her words but missed the memo. When she found out I was seeing someone after a long, long relationship, she said coldly, "I learned how to be alone, why can't you?" as if it were some badge of honor. How was it she survived so long without a passion for a person or thing except religion? How could she live without the miracles I have experienced, celebrated, and mourned? As I coaxed out a cork that was wedged in tightly, I knew that nothing was as important as love, and I knew that was why I was so compelled by wine. More than any other art form, wine and its vine are linked to happiness and heartbreak, to family, to nature, to humans trying to control the uncontrollable, just as we do in love.

Not quite ready to commit to drinking the wines— sometimes when you trip, it's hard to eat or drink until it is the right moment—I smelled. Swirled. Spat. The first wine was full of the smells of flowers tumbling into the spring. The second sip was my black lining. I continued to spit for a while, wanting to make sure to feel the wines on the intellectual spectrum. Finally, I got my nerve up and swallowed, just a little. The first wine was neither bitter nor cloying. It spoke of new but not slobbering attraction, with bounce and an excited, irregular heartbeat. The most amazing thing happened with the second, a wine from Campania made by a man I'd never met, Luigi Tecce. Deep stuff. I felt its earth, its grapes—aglianico— birthed from vines grown in the ancient soils around Pompeii, and I felt the volcano that birthed them, the majestic, catastrophic Vesuvius. I could sense a menacing cyclops running after a kid with skinned knees, and then it turned into a sweet goat, a whiff of paint thinner trailing behind. Leonard Cohen, full of soul and sonorous voice, with a dash of Tom Waits gravel. In the wine I saw hills of herbs, strong on rosemary and beach plum, basalt, and grit. And power.

I decided to open another, the one wine that I had been able to drink during the long days from winter into spring because it was more stone than fruit. A wine made like a sherry. I closed my eyes. This one I was used to. It was familiar. It wasn't tasking. And I realized the reason I had been craving it was for the salty minerality, as if I'd been lacking and my body had been yelling at me, "Take nourishment!" I have always had low blood pressure; the sherry was medicine after all.

In the morning, I lay in bed. I felt my face with my hands, my shoulders, my skin. I knew I wasn't 100 percent, but the feeling that there was a scratchy sweater under my skin was gone. Coffeed up, I tied on my mask, looping the stays behind my ears. I took a tote bag, and in the quiet, I walked to the greenmarket, where I stood in wonder at the flowers. Colors so saturated. I bought graceful lisianthus with lazy, bobbing heads. There were purple-spotted pinto potatoes and some green eggs from the Amish farmer. I walked home and called Peter on the way. I heard his voice and felt him. He was with me. I made new soup and realized that drinking alone was far from a hardship; it was a privilege, a luxury, and a teacher. Wine has been going strong for more than eight thousand years, since it was first made. Even if it sometimes failed to deliver at full sensorial capacity, I could still contemplate the people who made it, the vintage they made it in, and the natural disasters that had to be overcome to make something beautiful.

## DRINK THIS

Bodegas Gómez Nevado
Dorado Sierra Morena Seco
Grape: Airén, Palomino, Pedro Ximénez
Where: Andalucia, Spain

This is an amontillado style, still dry but deeper and richer than a fino. Fermented in tank, then into old amphora, where it settles, after which it heads into old barrel and winds its way through a solera for about fifteen years. Sherry lovers, get to work drinking this luscious wine of dry caramel with the salt pulled through it in threads. That acid? It's electric. This is the kind of deep contemplative wine that can get you through the winter.

At seven on any night in the spring of 2020, the city folk reached through their windows or, like me, climbed out on the fire escape, clanging on pots, punching bongos, clapping blocks. Then we retreated, and the curtains and blinds came down, the silence hushed the evening and night fell. As usual, I was in the mood for something to drink to help with the long darkness, but what? What would feel good? I had found that fruity and fresh wines hurt my mouth, and I couldn't figure out why. And then I realized what I wanted. Wines flooded with oxygen. Wines that were called oxidative. Wines of the Jura, wines from Jerez, and anything else made that way.

I stumbled on these antifruit variations back in 1998, in my food-reviewing days. Writing for *Paper* magazine, I was charged to write up Aquavit, a fancy joint in midtown where I'd never be able to go to on my own dime. I was in the mood for an unfamiliar white, and there it was. A region I was curious about. The Jura in France. I pointed to the "Vin jaune." I thought, A yellow wine? How odd.

I asked the sommelier what he thought of it. He told me it was a sauvignon; he smiled and brought it over. The color was indeed a little yellow-hued. I tasted and immediately said to my meat-eating boyfriend, Ronny, "This sucks."

He, who had turned into quite a good taster, wasn't sure what to make of it either. I had expected something green. Instead, we got something that tasted like a liquefied salt mine mixed with unsweetened caramel with a squeeze of lime and a dollop of lime pickle. This was pre-iPhone, and I couldn't Google it to find out what I was drinking. I whispered across the table, "He should have warned us, no?" I was too embarrassed to send it back. We shrugged. We drank.

Slowly. Then picked up the pace. Remarkably, by the end of the meal, we had polished off the bottle, lapping up every savory drop. Smitten? That was coming close to the way we felt about that Jacques Puffeney Vin Jaune.

Once at home, I heaved out my *Oxford Companion to Wine* and looked it up. Vin Jaune was made in a special way, allowed to stay in barrel without topping off for six years. As the volume evaporated and was exposed to more oxygen, the wine acquired something called a *voile* (veil), a naturally forming thick white layer of yeast. This sounded absolutely disgusting to me, in the way that *huitlacoche*—corn smut—sounded awful yet tasted divine.

I yelled to my beau, "No wonder it tasted weird."

He came to the living room and sat down.

"Did the sommelier say 'sauvignon'?" I asked him.

"I think so," he said.

"Well, the grape is called savagnin. And why didn't he tell us that a Vin Jaune was supposed to taste like sherry?"

"Because he didn't know either?"

Even though this was a full ten years before the wines from the Jura became a cult thing, even though they were a rarity, I felt that because I wrote about wine, I should have known. The feeling flushing through me was like those I had during old nightmares, showing up to fourth grade without having done my homework.

That was my entry into the universe of complex and salty oxidative wines and perhaps one of my most hard-to-admit moments about how ignorant I was.

Most table wines are made in reductive environments, meaning that oxygen is kept at bay to preserve the wine's freshness. Sherry and sherrylike wines like Vin Jaune are the opposite; they are oxidative wines. The wine is not protected from oxygen, and that allows stuff to happen. The layer of "flor" (yeast) eats the alcohol and releases acetaldehyde, which creates flavors that are particular to sherry and other flor-aged wines like nuts and dried fruits. The salinity inside the wines is concentrated, thus the ocean breeze. The flor also protects the wine from ruination—turning into vinegar. The transformation can be mind-bending stuff that super-glues the wines into memory. A Vin Jaune from the eighties drunk with friends after a tasting in Croatia. The intense brine, drenched with intensity and seashell of the Overnoy 2011 oxidative savagnin (whose wines have become legends). Years later, I can still salivate thinking about them.

And yet while the oxidative wines of Jura are the rage, and the older ones go for a pasha's ransom at wine auctions, their first cousin, sherry, cannot shed the out-of-fashion-grandma's-drink image. (My own grandmother Miriam drank Cherry Heering, something completely different.) The truth: Most sherry is dry.

Depending on the amount of aging, the result is varying degrees of exalted umami. As far as tingly acid, sherry never has as much nor is it as full-bodied as the Jurassic wines. But they are similar in profile nevertheless, and you should absolutely know that if you usually look for fruits and flowers in wine, go elsewhere. Because with these wines you're going to need to open your mind and mouth and be prepared for the bandage, dried fruit, nuts, and salt. And trust me, you can leave those bottles open for days, even weeks, and they will not be destroyed. That is the metaphor—the destruction is the wine's resurrection.

During the pandemic, I wanted the lightness yet depth of

sherry. Was it because oxygen was in our daily news? Tanks, tents, ventilators, monitors were constantly in my mind, and paradoxically, I was, craving a wine that could not be created without its presence. Was it a coincidence? Power of suggestion? Or was it something deeper, more primal?

The wine that spoke loudest to me during the darkest days was the Gómez Nevado. Inexpensive, it was sublime, savory, happy, pensive. It did the trick at 15 percent alcohol and gave me the needed buzz as the night came close in on me, but more than that, it just tickled something inside. The need to breathe.

## DRINK THESE OXIDATIVE WINES

You can certainly have red oxidative wines (hello, Madeira), but I was needing the edge and lightness of sherry. In the way that only wines from Champagne can be called champagne, only wines from the "Sherry Triangle"—the towns close to the Atlantic—can be called sherry. But oxidative wines are made all around the area, like the inland one from Gómez Nevado. From legal sherry-land, I especially love Fino or Manzanilla (essentially a Fino but made in a wave-battered town on the Atlantic, Sanlúcar de Barrameda); occasionally, a more viscous Oloroso or Palo Cortado does me well. From France, the Jura and Vin Jaune is quite expensive, but look for the words *sous voile* to find your oxidative savagnin, like a baby Vin Jaune and just delicious with some fruity Comté cheese.

There are oxidative wines (with a flor or without) all over the world, even Vermont, where Ms. Deirdre Heekin is playing around with the process. Vermont is new to this but looks promising.

Andalucia: Barbiana, Cota 45, Equipo Navazos, Fernando de Castilla, El Maestro Sierra, Bodegas Tradición, de la Riva, Gómez Nevado, Luis Perez, Bodegas Faustino González, Cruz Vieja, Bodegas Poniente, Williams & Humbert

Jura: (If you see *ouillé* on the label it means the bottle is topped off, so the oxidative effect is not as profound. Check the producers from the Jura chapter.)

Vermont: La Garagista Farm & Winery, Found Love

# Acknowledgments

This journey kicked off after my agent, Angela Miller, read a short essay I published in *New York* magazine and innocently emailed me an enthusiastic request, "I want a collection." The truth was that such a project was a deep-seated fantasy of mine for decades. In the end, this book was torn out of the pandemic's isolation grip, and I would be lying if I didn't confess to being indebted to my friends, relatives, and colleagues who pulled me out of lousy moods, snitty tantrums, and twisty sentences.

During the early part of the lockdown, my colleague Sue Shapiro, who presides over the writers' group I've been loyal to for about a decade and a half, was one of the few in my circle who would see me in person. Over the years her feedback has been sage. We survived the months with our masked walks, whether it was to find popcorn for her or bottles for me. I hatched out the book's structure as we clocked in our miles.

When the proposal was ready to be released into the world, my friend Lizzie Gilbert (no, not *that* Elizabeth Gilbert) had a hunch and matched me with editor Roz Lippel. Thus, the book found its dream home at Scribner. Working with Ms. Lippel and her subtle but firm direction was such a privilege. Also a big thank you to Kara Watson, who stepped in to see this book to the finish line with full (and much appreciated) talent and committment.

A round of thankful applause goes to those in the afore-mentioned group, my fabulous circle of pros, Haig Chahin-ian, Kate Walter, Lisa Lewis, Brenda Copeland, Nicole Bokat, Tony Powell, Amy Klein, Sybil Sage, Sharon Messmer, and Gabrielle Selz.

But there is support outside of the group. My trusty web-site editor on my *The Feiring Line* newsletter, Christy Frank, was always willing to read whatever I gave her; great at the bigger picture, she also has a deft ability to ground me.

My brilliant "French daughter," wine pro and beyond, Pas-caline Lepeltier, kept my facts straight. Bitch-and-moan ses-sions were almost daily with my German-based Australian friend, Felicity Carter, who continually gave me her blunt opinion, laser-sharp editing knife, and hysterical laughter at my fears. She always made me see the absurd humor side to a tragic moment. My old friend Liz Reisberg has been my longtime secret agent, whether for formatting or grammar or giving me zero tolerance for my indulgence in weird syntax. Liz has had her red pen out for every single one of my books. To my dear friend Ronni Olitsky for being an indefatigable cheerleader. Shout out to my cousin Madelyn Kelly for early essay readings and her feedback.

I am lucky enough to have a fairy godmother in the form of a "little sister." Melissa Clark has been such a close and dear friend for more than two decades. A truly evolved human being, she has never failed me when I needed her, whether it was hand-holding, opinions, or wisdom beyond her years. I can only hope I give to her as much as she gives to me. This also applies to José Pastor, who has hauled me out of so many ditches I can't count. This diablo has saintly generosity. From San Quentin to Seville and beyond, a bless-ing in my life. Love you for real.

# ACKNOWLEDGMENTS

A big thank-you goes to designer Natalia Oblinsky for taking my wish list for a book cover and making it come to beautiful life. To the whole team, you were a class act.

As with all of my previous books, I could never have done ronni it without the kindness, hospitality, and the work of the winemakers and vignerons who have pushed for wine to return to its authentic identity. To those who have shown me that wine is so much more than a drink with dinner, that it is soulful and a worthy life metaphor. There are way too many to mention, but these are the people, from France to Georgia to Chile to Italy, to Greece to Spain to Croatia and the United States who inspired me and handed me their stories to mesh with my own.

In addition, perhaps for this book more than ever, there were those people who believed in me before I knew writing was at all a possibility; from Judith Lynch (aka Piscatelli) in the ninth grade to the late, great poet Kofi Awooner who recognized something in me I denied, and to the and the late great poet Gerald Burns who not only taught me how to frail a banjo but sent my work out for publication behind my back, way before I could possibly identify with being a writer.

At the close of my second draft, I lost two of my inner circle, mentors, and friends, within weeks of each other. Becky Wasserman-Hone was the first. And as I wrap up these words it's hard not to fully embrace the irony that the memoir I was supposed to write was hers, not mine. As I write these notes of gratitude, a word I don't take lightly, I'm overwhelmed with sadness that this is a book she'll never read. This one, like all of mine, was started in her farmhouse, in the sweet hamlet under the jagged limestone cliffs, nourished by both Becky and her husband, Russell, emotionally and alimentarily. I'll miss her forever. And, Mr. Barbarino, a friend of our wilderness, I will miss his encouragement and being there for me always and the amazement and complete astonishment and reflection when confronting a vibrant wine. As always I miss my brother, Andrew. He was the real writer in the family. I fear my father got the short end of the stick in these pages, but I hope his eccentric character, even with some of the good, came out in the end. While imperfect, he gave me poetry. To PZ, thank you for understanding that I'm always working. I know it's difficult. And to my mother, #ethelwatch, thank you for being the best material a girl could have.

# About the Author

Journalist and essayist Alice Feiring was proclaimed "the queen of natural wines" by the *Financial Times*. Feiring is a recipient of a coveted James Beard Award for Wine Journalism, among many other awards. She has written for newspapers and magazines including the *New York Times, New York, Time, AFAR Magazine, World of Fine Wine,* and the beloved winezine *Noble Rot,* and has appeared frequently on public radio.

Her previous books include *Natural Wine for the People, The Dirty Guide to Wine, For the Love of Wine, Naked Wine: Letting Grapes Do What Comes Naturally,* and her controversial 2008 debut, *The Battle for Wine and Love: Or How I Saved the World from Parkerization.*

Alice lives in New York and publishes the authoritative natural wine newsletter, *The Feiring Line* (thefeiringline .com).